C000263181

FLASHBACKS NO.7

The Flashback series is sponsored by the
European Ethnological Research Centre,
c/o the National Museums of Scotland,
Chambers Street, Edinburgh EH1 1JF.

General Editor: Alexander Fenton

Frontispiece. Her Majesty Queen Elizabeth pays a wartime visit to Crathie church to open a sale of work. She is seen talking to Mary Ralph of the Women's Timber Corps. Mary sang in the choir. Photo: Mary Ralph (Mitchell).

TIMBER!

Memories of Life in the Scottish Women's Timber Corps, 1942–46

Affleck Gray

Edited by Uiga and John Robertson

TUCKWELL PRESS
in association with
The European Ethnological Research Centre

First published in Great Britain in 1998 by
Tuckwell Press
The Mill House
Phantassie
East Linton
East Lothian EH40 3DG
Scotland

Copyright © Uiga and John Robertson, 1998

All rights reserved

ISBN 1 86232 030 6

British Library Cataloguing in Publication Data
A Catalogue record for this book is available
on request from the British Library

Typeset by Hewer Text Ltd, Edinburgh
Printed and bound by Cromwell Press, Trowbridge, Wiltshire

This book is dedicated to that gallant band of young women from all walks of life in Scotland whose contribution to the war effort was immeasurable. To the memory of those who have passed away, and to those who have survived, many of whom, judging by their mobility and animation at the Reunions in recent years, might still be capable of swinging an axe or pulling a saw if the need arose, this belated account of the Corps is dedicated with a full sense of humility and appreciation for all their years of hard labour and cheerfulness against so many odds.

CONTENTS

ILLUSTRATIONS

by
Anne Shortreed

PLATES

CLARENCE HOUSE
S.W. 1

I remember so well the great contribution
made by the Women's Timber Corps in Scotland to
Victory in World War II.   No matter the conditions,
those in timber production worked tirelessly to aid
the war effort.   Their unsparing efforts earned our
gratitutde, and I would like here to pay my tribute
to these Lumber Jills.

Elizabeth R

Acknowledgements

Thanks are due to Bonny Macadam, Lundin Links, for advice and permission to reproduce so many of her photographs; Dorothy Kidd, Social Life Archive, National Museums of Scotland, Edinburgh; Doreen Butler, Lochgilphead; Jean Proctor, British Women's Land Army Society, Marple, Cheshire; The Forestry Commission, Edinburgh; Menzies Campbell, MP; Liz Brash, Royal Scottish Agricultural Benevolent Institution; Ann Wakeling, Aviemore; and to all who submitted their stories.

Special thanks are due to Irene Dallas who typed this document in her precious summer holidays.

Instead of writing her story Anne Shortreed, a former member of the Women's Timber Corps who was a trainer at Park House, Aberdeenshire, has done the delightful illustrations which greatly enhance the text. Special thanks to her also.

Affleck Gray in 1946, before leaving for Germany as a member of the Control Commission there.

Introduction
by Affleck Gray

Introduction to Wartime Timber Operations

Before the First World War the United Kingdom was, reputedly, the largest wood importing country in the world. Timber sources had been declining since the Middle Ages and had reached an all-time low in the wake of the Industrial Revolution. Home production covered only about five per cent of requirements and the UK became increasingly dependent on imports to meet the ever increasing need for wood. In peacetime this was no problem, but clearly in any war in Europe in which this country became involved, blockades would inevitably follow and the difficulties would become almost insuperable. For the armed forces alone, many trees would be required for building soldiers' living-quarters, mess and recreation rooms, for wooden crates for shipping clothing, food, armaments and ammunition; for converting into high explosives and gunstocks; and for building training planes and factories.

This was precisely what happened in the Great War and, in the emergency, home timber had to be ruthlessly requisitioned by Government. The necessary labour was severely reduced by reason of enlistment. In 1916 the British Government appealed to Canada to recruit a battalion of expert lumber men and send them across as soon as possible. In the spring of that year, the first draft of a Canadian Forestry Battalion arrived in this country and by October it was expanded into the Canadian Forestry Corps – the CFC. The Corps also operated in France and Spain. By Armistice Day the Corps was supplying about seventy per cent of the total timber used by the Allies on the Western Front and at that time there were about 12,000 CFC personnel in France and 10,000 in Britain.

The first cutting done by the CFC, in my native Speyside, was in the Sluggan Pass which runs from Kincardine Church to Loch Morlich. When the Canadians arrived in November 1916, they were housed in Glenmore Lodge, now a Youth Hostel, until they built their huts. A railway, supported on trestles in places, was constructed for two and a half miles down the Pass, along which some 50,000 trees were transported to the sawmill from whence the timber was conveyed on another light railway to the station at Aviemore. When I was young I remember looking for remnants of the rails.

Another larger timber operation, along the shores of Loch Morlich, transported around 76,000 trees from that area. Fortunately, the Duke of Richmond and Gordon had stipulated that a scattering of trees should be left to ensure natural regeneration. When the Sluggan operation finished the Canadian Company moved to the Nethy Forest, near Nethy Bridge, where some huge, very old trees were felled.

There is very little known about women working in the woods during World War 1 but there did exist in Scotland at least one small group which was sponsored by the Duke of Atholl and accommodated in the old inn at Inver, Dunkeld, which had been turned into flats. It was referred to as The Ladies' Forestry Corps.

Three members of the group were involved in a drowning tragedy in the River Tay in 1918, casting a gloom over the whole community where the girls were very popular. It appears that, without mentioning their intention to anyone, they went to bathe in a dangerous pool, known locally as the Rock Pool, about one mile above Dunkeld.

Bill Edwards, a local man, vividly remembers the bodies of the girls being taken to Inver in an Estate cart after being recovered from the river by members of the Newfoundland Forestry Corps who were cutting timber at Craig Vinean nearby.

In May 1917 the Board of Agriculture (Scotland) applied to

Introduction

Government for the sum of £2000 to recruit 200 women for forestry work in Scotland. The estimated expenditure was:

Outfits @ £3	£600.00
Maintenance grants for instruction for 3 weeks @ 10/- per week	£450.00
Travelling expenses to and from work 100 women for 20 weeks @ 5/- per week	£100.00
Railway warrants (double journey) 100 women @ £1.00	£100.00
Payment during unemployment – 200 women at an average of 12 days unemployment	£300.00

Although little has been discovered about the involvement of women in timber work at that time, I distinctly recall that, when I was a young boy, women 'tailed' (guided the end of the logs towards the saw blade) at sawmills and burned brushwood. Women, however, worked on the land in large numbers. In 1917 Roland Protheroe, who was then Minister of Agriculture, became so concerned about our dwindling food supplies, due to so many farm labourers being called up for active service, that he created the Women's Land Army and thousands of young women from all walks of life flocked to the nearest registration office to enrol. Their valiant efforts to feed the nation have been well documented elsewhere. A smaller number was allocated to timber operations but remained under the umbrella of the Department of Agriculture.

The story was repeated when World War II broke out. We were faced with the same dilemma over timber and once more the British Government appealed for overseas assistance. The Ministry of Supply recruited over two thousand lumberjacks from Newfoundland in 1939 and 1940 who were accommodated in some thirty camps in Scotland and England. They were civilians and paid as such. Five hundred timber men were raised in British Honduras and I recall a camp of these men at Backies on Dunrobin Estate when I was engaged on Acquisitions work, valuing requisitioned timber there. I think, however, that the climate was so unsuitable for them, and they suffered so much illness, that they had to be returned home. In a speech in the House of Lords calling for a separate Forestry Commission for Scotland to deal with what would inevitably be a massive amount of reafforestation, the Duke of Sutherland referred to the recruitment of men from a tropical climate to the north of Scotland as 'sheer lunacy'! Military units were also sent from Australia and New Zealand to work in the forests.

The Canadian Forestry Corps

The initial request to the Canadian Government in October 1939 resulted in a new Canadian Forestry Corps. Many of those who volunteered were veterans of World War I, including the Corps Commander, Brigadier-General J. B. White. The camps in Scotland numbered thirty, each with a large complement of men, extending from Skibo in Sutherland down to Glentanar, Banchory and Mar Lodge on Deeside, south to Strathspey and Blair Atholl and west to Inveraray.

The financial agreement between the British and Canadian Governments was that Canada was to bear the cost of pay, allowances, personal equipment, pensions and the cost of transport to and from the UK. The British Government was to pay for all other services, equipment and maintenance. Canada provided and paid for medical officers but, if hospital fees were incurred, the British would meet the costs. Timber operations were organised by British authorities through the Home Grown Timber Department of the Ministry of Supply. This unusual arrangement seemed to work fairly smoothly.

Initially, twenty companies arrived in 1940, drawn from all over Canada, followed by a further ten in 1941. They all received military training in Canada before embarking from Halifax, in Nova Scotia, for the hazardous crossing of the Atlantic and their destination on the Clyde. From there the men were sent to various camps, mainly in the Scottish Highlands.

They brought with them equipment which was far more up to date than that in current use in Britain: TD9 caterpillars, lorries, bulldozers and diesel saw-mills. The men lived in camps of wooden huts and, sometimes, Nissen huts. A cookhouse, mess, ablutions with hot showers (to the envy of our girls!) and recreation huts were attached to most camps, with separate quarters for sergeants and for officers. The Atholl Arms Hotel in Blair Atholl was used for a time as officers' quarters. As the camps were often on estate land, electricity was usually available and at Mar Lodge camp the Canadians installed their own generator.

Five camps were situated in Strathspey, six on Deeside and two in Blair Atholl but the main concentration was around the Moray and Dornoch Firths, where both the Lovat and Skibo estates each had five camps. In Strathspey, I had many dealings with the Canadians and was most interested in their machinery and equipment and realised that their techniques would be copied in Britain in post-war years. The companies were usually divided into two sections: one for felling and the other for working the saw-mill. The Canadians, like the Newfoundlanders, logged their trees leaving knee-high stumps and had to be persuaded that this was not our method! They also hated the Scottish weather: rain and more rain and then snow which prevented effective evacuation of timber. However, their bulldozers and lorries were fitted with snow ploughs which were invaluable for clearing both their own roads and even the main roads in the Highlands. A remark from a Canadian forester working in Caithness was recorded in his diary, 'The last tree of commercial value left standing in Caithness was felled today at 15.45 hours and three cheers were given by the men!'

As in the First War, the Canadians had an almost immediate harmonious rapport with the Scottish people which endured throughout their service. They were welcomed with open arms and showered with invitations to dances, whist drives, concerts and into people's homes and, when their own recreation halls were constructed, the locals were warmly invited to the entertainment they laid on, including invitations to wine and dine in their mess rooms. Many of them married Scottish girls.

The Home Grown Timber Production Department

When war with Nazi Germany appeared to be inevitable, the Government set in motion the machinery to deal with all foreseeable contingencies. With regard to timber imports, which would undoubtedly suffer from blockade, we would have to depend largely on our own resources again.

In 1937 the Forestry Commission, in conjunction with the Board of Trade, started to draw up plans for felling timber in the event of war. To maintain a home supply three categories were identified: woods which could be felled immediately, woods which could be felled if necessary: and woods which could be felled only in extreme need. The Home Grown Timber Advisory Committee was then established in 1939 at the outbreak of war. At this point the Forestry Commission was divided into two divisions: the Forest Management Department, to carry on normal work, and the Timber Supply Department, to deal with war needs. In 1941 the responsibility for timber production was given to the Home Grown Timber Production Department of the Ministry of Supply.

Introduction

Those of us who were in the employment of the Forestry Commission, and had been specially selected for immediate transfer to timber production, were alerted well in advance that, in the event of war, we would be required to pack all our goods and chattels and be prepared to move immediately to our designated stations in any part of the country where we would be responsible for the production of timber of all categories for war and civil purposes – railway sleepers and crossing ties, sawn mining timbers, pit props, telegraph poles and poles for planting on beaches to thwart enemy landings by sea or air.

The Newfoundland Forestry Unit

Immediately war was declared, I moved into a house at Ardross in Easter Ross with my family and became responsible for all timber operations north of Dingwall, including the very first contingent of the Newfoundland Forestry Unit (NFU). They were a tough bunch of men who built their own log cabins, stuffing the gaps with moss to exclude draughts. Later, the Ministry of Health objected to these primitive constructions and we had to erect hutted accommodation with ablutions and toilets, dining rooms and drying rooms. To my horror, the 'Newfies', as they came to be known, felled the trees at knee level and I had to read the riot act at such a waste of timber! About 10 am, they all downed tools and said, 'We've got to go to camp for a lunch'. They seemed to call every meal a 'lunch'. So, off they trooped to the camp and began diving into the pots for cold lumps of beef, encased in a layer of fat, which they wolfed down ravenously giving them severe stomach cramps. No wonder I had the Alness doctor in constant attendance! However, once they were used to our way of working, I got on very well with them, although I was much relieved when Colonel Cullen, with two other officers, came over and took that responsibility off my shoulders. The Newfoundland record of timber production throughout the war was very high.

There were various Newfoundlander camps in the north of

Timber!

Scotland, several of which were in Speyside, so I came across the men again when I worked there. The Company at Carrbridge was billeted in the village hall until they constructed their camp of log cabins, near the golf course. There were others at Dell Farm, Nethybridge, Auchernack, near Grantown-on-Spey, Grainish, Aviemore and at Laggan. It is still possible to trace the concrete bases on which these camps stood.

Carrbridge had one of the largest timber yards in the Highlands and became one of the busiest stations, from which as many as 600 wagon-loads were known to be transported in one day. This was the result of having both Newfie units and Ministry of Supply men working along with Women's Timber Corps.

Many of the Newfies had never seen a car when they arrived in this country from the backwoods of Newfoundland and I recall the incongruous sight of grown men learning to ride a bicycle around Carrbridge.

They were very sociable, putting on dances, concerts and film shows in their recreation huts to which the local people were invited and, like the Canadians, many married Scottish girls.

A report in the *Inverness Courier* in 1942 states that a successful dance was held in the Recreation Room of Lumber Camp No.1 at Moy, near Inverness. The event raised the sum of £10:16/- for the Spitfire Fund. The aim was to purchase a Spitfire to bear the name 'Newfoundland' and, if possible, to be piloted by a Newfoundlander. To date the sum raised in Newfoundland camps throughout the country was £1730. But the article does not state how much a Spitfire would cost!

In September 1942, the Deputy Prime Minister, Clement Attlee, went to watch the Newfies at work in Aberdeenshire. After lunch in their dining hut, he thanked them for the work they were doing for the war effort and said it was greatly appreciated by the Government.

Introduction

The Women's Timber Corps

In any introduction to the wartime operations of the Women's Timber Corps (WTC) it is hardly possible to dissociate the prodigious war effort of the Corps from the equally massive contribution of the Women's Land Army (WLA), the one in the forests providing timber for war and civil purposes, the other on the land feeding the nation at a time when woodcutters and farm labourers were called up for active service. It is, of course, no surprise to find that women worked in the forest and on the land. Most farmer's wives and families, kitchen maids and dairy maids had always had their seasonal occupations in addition to routine work, particularly at harvest time: stooking sheaves, lifting potatoes (tattie howking), berry picking, topping turnips (heuking neeps) and similar tasks.

Women had always found occupations in the forest, gathering cones for seed and working in nurseries. This work was frequently carried out by the travelling people who were paid by the bushel when their bags of cones were brought to the nursery for kilning and winnowing. There was, however, no nation-wide organisation, as in the First War, until the outbreak of war in 1939 when farms and forests were seriously depleted of manpower.

It was at Ardross that I first encountered members of the Women's' Timber Corps (WTC). Many of the girls came from Lewis, Harris, Skye, Mull and other parts of the west with a leavening of local girls. At first, they were treated with some derision and ribaldry by the male strength and were regarded as more ornamental than useful. Even the Operations foreman held the same views as the men. I, however, with recollections of girl students in the Aberdeen University Mountaineering Club, with their ability to climb as sturdily as the boys and their capacity to portage heavy back-packs to a high-level camp, had other ideas and counselled a 'Wait and see policy'. 'Perhaps', I added, 'you may be in for a big surprise.' How soon I was to be vindicated! In a very short time, male chauvinism received a very thick ear when the girls

9

demonstrated that they could play the woodcutters at their own game and even outplay them in some departments. After two years on Production, I succeeded Andrew Crawford as Acquisitions Officer for the North Division, based in Inverness, and had further experience of the hardiness of the WTC.

In June 1939, when the WLA was resuscitated some experienced women, still active enough, volunteered for service along with thousands of young women nation-wide, who again came from all walks of life.

The organisation was again run entirely by women. Lady Denman – subsequently honoured with a DBE for her services to the war effort – was an Honorary Director with her home, Balcombe Place, becoming the Headquarters of the WLA. This was by agreement with the War Cabinet, the Ministry of Labour, the National Farmers' Union and the National Union of Agriculture Workers. The Agriculture Wages Board dealt with the question of wages. Estimates had to be submitted annually to the Treasury and included costs of training, uniform, hostel and travelling expenses. The requisitioning of hostels was dealt with by the Ministry of Labour and Works. Committees were organised separately and each County had its Organising Secretary and Local Representative who had the onerous duty of dealing tactfully with all manner of personal difficulties the members might have in adjusting to a new way of life.

Uniform consisted of brown breeches, a rather smart fawn jersey, fawn duffel coat, brown shoes and knee-length woollen stockings, dungarees, oilskins, a sou'wester and a jaunty little fawn round hat bearing a badge with a motif of a sheaf of wheat.

Mavis Williams, author of that splendid, hilarious and revealing book 'Lumber Jill', recalls that in the course of her interview for the WLA she was informed that she would be wasted there but, with her qualifications, she should consider the new Corps which was being formed for which a slightly higher academic qualification was required. This was a new venture inaugurated by the Ministry of Supply. And that, in April 1942, was the beginning of the famous **WOMEN'S**

TIMBER CORPS – WTC – in England. Soon, they had a separate identity, although closely related to the WLA; the fawn jersey was replaced with green and the round hat with a green beret carrying the WTC badge and a spruce tree motif instead of a wheatsheaf. Scotland followed quickly with the inauguration of its **WOMEN'S TIMBER CORPS** in May 1942. In Scotland the registration of recruits was done at Women's Land Army Headquarters. They were then seconded for training and employment to the **Ministry of Supply (Home Grown Timber Department)** which, thereafter, assumed responsibility for the administration of the **Scottish Women's Timber Corps** under the Essential Works (General Provisions) Order, 1942. The Parliamentary responsibility for the welfare of both the WTC and the WLA lay with the Secretary of State for Scotland.

The wage for entrants at seventeen years was 35/-, for age eighteen, 41/6d and, for nineteen years and over, the weekly wage was 46/-. If hutting or other accommodation was provided, then a payment of 3/- per week was charged. The girls were entitled to one week's paid holiday per year and, if off sick, they got one week's full pay and board and lodging paid for the remainder of the illness.

The Dreaded Munitions

In the spring of 1941 Ernest Bevin, Minister of Labour and National Service in the war cabinet, declared that one million wives were wanted for war work. Inconveniences, he said, would have to be suffered and younger women would have to leave their homes and go where their services were required. He asked for a million women, either full-time or part-time, to work in munitions or in shops and offices in order to release younger, more mobile women to fill shells and make munitions.

Mr Bevin hinted that more compulsion than the British people had ever known might have to be carried out to win the struggle. It would be better to suffer temporarily than to be in perpetual slavery to the Nazis. The age reservation rule would be replaced by individual reservation and employers would have to make accurate returns of those in their employ. He said that everyone would have to 'heave together'.

Tom Johnston, Secretary of State for Scotland, indicated in May, 1942 that the numbers of girls being posted south of the border to munitions factories had decreased. But, by September, 1942 Scottish Members of Parliament, from all parties, had begun to realise that the transfer of girls to work in munitions was not a sensible idea and should be stopped. They requested a meeting with Mr Bevin to discuss the matter. Scottish girls from the cities were not always as badly affected as the girls from rural areas and the islands but all the girls should have expected a sympathetic hearing. In war-time it is necessary to accept that circumstances are far from normal but the parents of these girls, sent to work in huge factories far from home, were most unhappy about their daughters' welfare.

Surely it would have been possible to establish munitions factories in Scotland and stop the mass transfer of girls to England. But, it was to avoid munitions work that many girls opted to stay in Scotland and work either on the land, in the Women's Land Army, or join the Women's Timber Corps and work in the forests.

In August 1942, Mr Barbour, labour director under the Ministry of Fuel and Power, said that no case could be made for withholding women's labour from the collieries. Every able-bodied man, he said, should be released from the pit-head, as women were quite able to take their place! Jobs which could be undertaken by women included labouring at the pit-head, loading pit props into hutches to go down the mine and cleaning the coal on the screening plant. Women could also take over from the bing workers, removing the refuse.

How much better off were the WTC members working in the clean air of the forests, providing the props to go down the mines.

Introduction

Schoolboys, Teachers and Undergraduates

Even schoolboys, teachers and undergraduates worked in the woods during the summer holidays. In July 1940 a party of twenty-one pupils, aged fourteen to seventeen, felled, measured and cross-cut four thousand five hundred cubic feet of timber, burned over twenty acres of brushwood and helped in the construction of a bridge. About fifteen poles between seventeen and twenty feet long were loaded on to each truck and subsequently transferred to railway wagons. However, it was not an entirely successful scheme and was abandoned fairly quickly. Due to the inexperience of the volunteers little care had been taken to clear the sites after felling and the resulting tangle of branches often had to be cleared up by their successors.

I trust that the following selection of stories, sent to me by former WTC members, will provide a feeling for, and clear impression of, what life was like for the girls in the Women's Timber Corps.

Affleck Gray

FOOTNOTE

Before Affleck Gray's death in 1996 he wrote that he would be continuing to press the Government about representation of the Women's Timber Corps at Armistice Services and other public occasions.

When Affleck Gray died in 1996 his work on this book was unfinished. It had been his intention to write a history of the WTC augmented by reminiscences from the members. Since his death, his daughter, Uiga Robertson, and his grandson, John Robertson, have produced this volume from his papers and hope that it fulfils his wish to highlight the contribution of these ladies to the war effort.

FELLING

This extract from Meet the Members, *a collection of remi-niscences published in 1946, was written by Marjory Stark who was a Trainer at Shandford Lodge and sadly died in 1994.*

Felling, the process of cutting down trees, is one of the most interesting and highly skilled jobs done by the Women's Timber Corps. Good felling is a matter of knowledge and judgement and good fellers are fascinating to watch. There are men who have been at this job for a dozen years or more who will admit that they can still learn new things about it.

The first part of this process, and the most difficult to learn, is what we in Scotland call 'laying-in'. This is the preliminary axe work: levelling off butress roots and cutting a 'mouth' in the tree on the side to which you want it to fall, generally the 'front' or clear side. We of the Scottish Timber Corps have been felling and laying-in for all the time the WTC has existed here, and some of the girls have been doing it for longer. We generally use a four and a half pound axe, though some girls use heavier and some lighter axes. We mostly work on pitwood trees, though some work on bigger stuff.

Having prepared your tree, you next 'throw' it or, in other words, saw it off root. This brings me to a difference of opinion. In the south of Scotland, right up as far as Perthshire and Angus, it is customary to kneel at the side of your tree when sawing it off root. In fact professional wood-cutters wear kneeling pads strapped to their knees all day when they are felling. But, in the north it is customary to stand and stoop to your saw as you throw trees. It is all a matter of preference.

MN

20th November, 1945

Miss Stark and the girls at Bowmont Camp

T.C. D/1/DS

The Deputy Director has asked me to send you an extract from the letter which he received from the proprietors of Bowmont Forest Estate.

"I have pleasure in accepting the area back felled by you and in doing so would remark that a splendid job has been made of the clearing and burning."

The Deputy Director specially asks that I will congratulate the forewoman and members of the W.T.C. and tell them how much he appreciates the praise which the Department has got chiefly through the work of the Women's Timber Corps.

Dudley Simpson

Chief Officer W.T.C.
(Scotland)

However, it is most important to have a light grip of the saw, to swing your arms easily and rhythmically from the shoulders, never to pull your saw and always, if at all possible, to use its full length. The type of saw generally used is a cross-cut with detachable handles so that it may be removed from the cut after the wedge is driven in, should this prove necessary. The wedge is driven in if the tree is leaning back or pressing on the saw or if it is taking too long about falling and it is becoming unsafe to go on sawing. If the difficult tree is large, a rope is sometimes attached to a limb or branch beforehand, either by means of a long pole or by climbing the tree, and a good pull on this brings the tree down where you want it.

The final process in felling is 'snedding'. I know no other word for this. It means cutting off the branches and the top of the tree. Some people prefer a small two and a half pound axe for this. You work right up your tree, taking off all the branches you can reach, and generally cut the top off where the tree is about two and a half inches in diameter. The tree is turned using a cant-hook or peevie tool with a hinged hook designed for the purpose and the process is repeated. The last job is to pile the branches or to burn them.

This is by no means the whole story, or the whole secret of felling, it is merely an attempt to give a rough idea of one of the jobs done by the Women's Corps. As I remarked at the beginning, felling is a highly skilled and interesting job and I think quite a few of us will be rather sorry when the time comes to give it up, even if it does mean that better days have come.

MEMORIES

BONNY MACADAM

If you can do better Macadam, swop with Jimmy!

Two things that interested me more than any others were motor mechanics and anything to do with trees and plants. Having been brought up on a small estate, I was accustomed to using axes and saws to help provide firewood for the house and, at the age of ten, could strip down a baby Austin 7 with only a little help from my much older brother!

In 1938, expecting war to be inevitable, I trained as a motor mechanic, obtained my Public Service Vehicle (PSV) licence, drove buses and lorries and, for a time, was part of a female convoy group taking vehicles, built in Edinburgh, to army and R.A.F. depots in England.

In July 1942 there was an advertisement in The Scotsman appealing for girls to join a new unit of the Women's Land Army called the Women's Timber Corps. The word timber was enough for me! After being questioned by a Miss Cameron in my home in Dunbar, I had to wait and wonder for over a month before getting my membership card on 29th August. I was told to be in Waverley station to catch a train for Brechin and was pleasantly surprised to find several other girls on the same journey.

We were met in Brechin by our boss, Robert Allison, who had been recalled from the Argyll and Sutherland High-landers in order to set up a camp to train girls in all branches of forestry at Meiklour, between Perth and Blairgowrie. However, so many girls volunteered for training that he had to move to larger premises at Shandford Lodge, a shooting lodge with enough space to erect several army huts in the garden. Shandford Lodge, eight miles from Brechin on

Off to work

the Kirriemuir road, was requisitioned for war-time use and was run by a Commandant, Mrs Gosling, an ex-WAAF, along with a matron, Miss Bonar, a cook, Madge Leckie and some girls who had volunteered for cooking and cleaning. Later Mrs Gosling was replaced by Jessie Cameron who had interviewed girls in Edinburgh two years previously. Miss MacConnell was a monthly visitor, employed to oversee all women's camps.

A few girls were made trainers straight away as they had been in the Women's Forestry Service, the forerunner of the Timber Corps, and were capable of showing us how to use a saw and an axe correctly. Mr Allison was a very strict chief instructor who was determined to turn out WTC members fit to be posted anywhere in Scotland, to any timber camp or to any forester who needed extra help. The WTC was part of the Ministry of Supply, our full title being Home Grown Timber Production Department, HGTPD – MOS – quite a mouthful!

At Shandford there was a huge old oak wood surrounded by young pine trees; an ideal place for training. We were all taught to fell the trees with axe and cross-cut saw, sned, then drag the trees with horse or tractor to the sawmill. The end product was milled timber and pit-props, all in great demand for the coal mines and the beaches.

It was a very tough life: wearing hard, leather boots, swinging heavy axes and living in stark army huts. Breakfast was at seven o' clock: porridge, bread, margarine and tinned pilchards in tomato sauce, which I have never eaten since! Once, for a treat, I sent to our family Malt Extract Company for a hundredweight of malt extract which, at least, was sweet. When we returned from the woods at five o' clock a filling meal awaited us. Madge worked wonders with the rations!

Badly blistered heels and hands were the order of the day, aching backs from being bent double for a good part of each day and wearing still damp clothes from the previous day were all overcome by the good spirits of the girls and the feeling that it was all in a good cause, doing our bit for the war effort.

Timber!

I was lucky to be kept on as a trainer after the month's tuition. As I had been to a 'posh' school, I had to take a lot of teasing from the girls. An incident which sticks in my mind is coming upon a certain cheeky girl, who always imitated me, standing quite forlorn, leaning on her axe, no doubt with blistered hands. On being asked how she was, she gave the reply I truly deserved, 'Jings! A'm that bloody happy!'

Those of us who lived in the house were luckier than the girls in the huts in the rose garden who slept in bunk beds, had to learn how to cope with Tilly paraffin lamps and had to visit the cold ablution hut where there was nothing as luxurious as hot water!

Waiting to drop a load of bottoming from my tipper lorry, I watched a driver trying to reverse an articulated pole wagon up to the sawmill and was overheard by Mr Allison to say that I could do it better myself! Imagine my horror when a voice from behind me said, 'Macadam, if you can do better, you can jolly well swop with Jimmy'. I was sorry that I had not kept quiet as, from then on, I became the pole wagon driver! I had to teach other girls to drive the smaller vehicles and deliver timber to several stations: sometimes loads of pit-props and sometimes bigger timber needed for desert warfare. Once we got the knack of lifting timber we were able to lift weights along with any man, as our muscles were really impressive!

Around that time a trainee, Mary, was being taught by 'Crolly', Betty Croll, to feed the big saw with huge trees and was told why she should never wear gloves. Unfortunately, she forgot this good advice and one day a log caught in her glove and carried her hand into the saw. Mr. Allison's wife, Meg, who was a nurse, came immediately and wrapped the poor hand in a towel. Then Bob Allison and I rushed the girl off to Brechin hospital, carefully taking the severed finger with us. We tried to keep up Mary's spirits on the way by telling stories and were amazed when she asked if she could tell us one. This involved a man who had been off work from a sawmill and was asked on his return what had happened. He replied "Och I just did that. Oh no! there's another finger away'. I think our laughter was tinged with a touch of hysteria!

Another of my jobs was to convey the girls to Brechin or Kirriemuir to dances. Taking them there was easy but, when it came to 'round-up' time, trying to collect the correct number was a different story! It reminds me of when I was shepherding after the war and sending my collie to look for strays. The only difference was that I had no collie then!

I remember an occasion when I had a German prisoner of war as second man on my lorry and we needed petrol from the pumps at the Finavon Hotel, which also had a very friendly public bar. A number of my friends used to quench their thirst there and were always willing to 'stand their hand' to a then, young and slim WTC girl. Of course, I thought that Mr Allison was miles from Finavon, so I handed over the precious keys of the lorry to the German, telling him to fill up while I nipped into the bar. But that was the very day that Mr Allison changed his plans and appeared in search of petrol! Bob, as I have known him all these years, still remembers what he had to say to Macadam for leaving her lorry.

From Shandford, which I greatly missed, I was posted to a camp at Kirriemuir on Kinnordy Estate, near Glamis. There I lived in a hut for the first time and realised how cold it became on winter nights. It was not unusual for hot-water bottles to freeze! Instead of undressing to go to bed we piled on all our dry clothes, while the wet, working clothes steamed round the wood-burner.

My last winter in WTC was bitterly cold. I think this accounted for the rheumatic fever with which I landed in hospital. Mrs Stoddart, Red Cross, asked me to stay and help her in the Bank house when I was discharged. There, I spent a very happy recuperation.

One Saturday morning the Red Cross was having a practice with the Ambulance Service and Mrs Stoddart asked if I would act as hostess to Lady X who was coming to open proceedings. A woman came to the door long before Lady X was expected so I invited her in and passed the time of day until, looking at my watch, I said, 'Excuse me, but I am expecting a 'dear old trout' any minute now and must go and look for her.' I was shattered when she said, with a definite twinkle in her eye, 'You're Bonny who drives the huge wagon, aren't you? Well, you don't have to go. The 'dear old trout' is right here.' How I wished to be in my polewagon at that moment!

After that I went to the Orkney Islands to drive a NAAFI van for a Royal Naval Service camp and remained till the war finished.

I had a variety of jobs in the post war years including farming near Hawick, when I learned a lot about lambing and shepherding. I was also a director in the family malt business, British Malt Products, until it was sold.

My Timber Corps days were some of the best in my life. I still enjoy meeting several friends each month and our tongues never stop saying 'Do you remember . . . ?' I hope that this publication will bring our great war effort to the fore and we will no longer be the 'Forgotten Corps'.

CHRIS TURNER
(NÉE MACDONALD)

We had to scrape the mouse droppings off the butter!

In the spring of 1940 I, along with a colleague, received calling up papers. We were both qualified hairdressers but, as hairdressing was classed as a luxury, we had to register for war service.

We went along to the local recruiting office and offered our services as hairdressers in the WAAF. We were informed, however, that timber measurers were more urgently required in the Ministry of Supply Home Grown Timber Production Department. Being young and enthusiastic to do our bit for 'King and Country', we duly reported to the appropriate office in Church Street, Inverness. After interview, we had a brief medical and both of us were then accepted as suitable 'timber fodder'. We spent approximately one week in the office discussing maps, how to work out the cubic contents of a tree and hence an area of standing timber. That was our sole office training; there remained the field training, and we little imagined what was involved in all that!

The next morning, our Acquisitions Officer took us by car to a wood about thirty miles from Inverness and, armed with scribing knives for marking the trees, girthing tapes for measuring, and, of course, note books and pencils, we started out upon our new career. Having been shown which trees to mark in a thinning – in a clear fell every tree had to be counted – we proceeded to quarter the wood from one end to the other, calling out 'Scots Pine' so much, 'Larch' so much until we were quite hoarse and so glad when lunch time arrived. By the end of the day we were very tired and hungry

25

after walking miles. So different from the comforts of the Salon! It took us about two weeks to complete this assignment, travelling by car each day. On our next job we had to stay away from home. Some of the accommodation was crude in the extreme, but not this one at Spinningdale in Sutherland. It was a delightful log cabin, loaned to us by Skibo Estate, situated in a lovely glade in the middle of the woods surrounding the Fairy Glen. A stream tumbled over rocks at the front door and the log cabin itself was fitted with all the civilised amenities. But alas! We were there for only a very short time before journeying westwards to Achnacarry Estate, the seat of Cameron of Lochiel and, at the time, a Commando training ground.

The accommodation at Achnacarry was a rat-infested bothy above stables. It was filthy and unhygienic beyond description. In bed, we could hear the rats scratching and squeaking in the walls. In the daytime, it was even worse! For cooking and heating we had an archaic grate with a huge black kettle sitting on the hob. It was so heavy we couldn't lift it full from the water supply downstairs so, to fill it, we had to go up and down stairs for jugfuls of water. Before we descended, however, we always took the precaution of banging on the stairs to disperse the rats to their holes. Sanitation was primitive; a filthy little shed in the yard without water and no place to have a bath or even a proper wash. We had to make do with an old zinc bath about two feet long and a foot wide, and some juggling! The only privacy was downstairs amongst the rats, and that, of course, was by prior arrangement! I used to sing as loudly as I could, to frighten them off, until my so-called ablutions were completed.

One of our projects at Achnacarry was to assess the volume of timber along the shores of Loch Arkaig and to get there we had to travel by boat, sometimes in the inexperienced hands of our Senior Officer. However, the Achnacarry Forester accompanied us on this particular job. He knew something about boats and that gave us a little more confidence on a loch which was subject to sudden squalls. The assessment of

Glen Mallie Wood at Achnacarry was the principal job and it was a tough assignment for five young girls.

The old open Scots Pine wood was rough with boulders and, in places, covered with long rank heather and riven with deep ravines which had to be negotiated with caution. Also, the Commandos, who were in training at Achnacarry at the time, had inadvertently set fire to an area of our wood. So, to add to our physical tests of endurance, we had to contend with burned trees which, on close contact, made us as black as chimney sweeps.

A good deal of time was spent journeying to and from the wood on foot and, as we approached the far end, the 'boss', in his wisdom, put it to us that we might cut down the long trudge each day and night by vacating the Achnacarry 'palace' and taking up residence in an empty cottage near the head of the Glen. We all readily agreed, if only to get away from the rats. Arrangements were made with the estate factor to flit our beds and bedding, pots and pans, by horse and cart to the cottage.

When we arrived there, we discovered that the Commandos had been in residence and left the cottage in a sad state. Straightaway, we set to and tried to make the place as habitable as possible. No conveniences, of course, not even a latrine, but there was a fine stream nearby and for that we were truly thankful! Now we could bathe each night and cleanse ourselves of the day's dirt and sweat. Talk about back to nature! We now knew something of the life style of a cave woman! The 'boss' was a man of sensitivity and consideration and discreetly stayed indoors at 'bath' time. It was primitive in all conscience, but it was a beautiful spot and we thoroughly enjoyed our stay there, despite all the shortcomings.

We did our own catering and had to do our shopping in Fort William which took most of Saturday as the bus service was very limited. Incidentally, we took it in turn to do the cooking and each day one member remained behind so that a meal was ready for the return of the slave labour each night. Fortunately, it was summertime when we were at Achnacarry and the scenery was really beautiful, but we didn't shed any tears on leaving the place.

It is so long ago that I cannot recall in which order our Acquisition of woods came but I do remember moving from the sublime to the ridiculous. When we were told that we would be staying in an hotel for two weeks, we were over the moon. Baths, meals, no chores! Oh the joy of it! Alas, by the end of the week, we realised that we would actually be out of pocket because pay and subsistence allowance were so derisory. But we made the most of it.

There were usually five or six girls in one squad. They came mainly from shops or offices and they were, on the whole, a jolly lot. They had to be!

I remember we were sent to a little hamlet called Contin which is just outside Dingwall in Ross-shire. We had the use of an empty cottage, again lacking in all facilities. There were no food cupboards but fruit crates, standing on end, were made to serve the purpose. In the morning, when we started to prepare breakfast, we had to scrape the mouse droppings off the butter before we could use it!

A flush toilet was too much to expect and we had to endure a latrine consisting of a rough wooden frame over a bucket. We had to take turns of hauling the filthy bucket down to the river and cleaning it. It was really a disgusting job for young girls, unaccustomed to such a primitive way of life.

Our civilian clothing was rapidly beginning to fall apart after months of ploughing through woods, in some cases prickly spruce, burned heather and high bracken. Also, the rough terrain had taken toll of our footwear. In desperation, I bought myself a pair of knee length leather boots for the inflated price of five pounds which was one pound more than a week's wages. The boots were not really very suitable because we had so much water to wade through, but, having spent so much on them, I just had to wear them out! We did eventually succeed in getting some odd – odd being the operative word – rubber boots which were Canadian Army surplus and filled them up with numerous pairs of socks. We looked like a band of nomads, and probably smelled accordingly. Our friends were not impressed! Thus, although we were inadequately clothed and shod, winter descended upon us and it was far from being pleasant. I recall one of the older girls crying with the pain in her semi-frozen fingers.

The Women's Timber Corps was unformed and not yet officially recognised and, if I recall correctly, it was early in 1943 before we were supplied with uniforms. That was a tremendous blessing. The comfort was unbelievable after our make-shift, civilian rig-outs on which, of course, we had to expend our clothing coupons.

When Acquisition came to an end in 1943, some of us were transferred to office work for which we had no previous training. One simply reported to the Foreman in charge of a timber operations unit, was shown what to do and politely told to get on with it. I was in an office with another girl near Evanton, a village in Ross-shire. We had quite a large pay roll and much form filling for timber despatches by rail to coal mines, the Army and other users of timber. The Army required many poles for setting up on beaches against the possibility of parachute landings by the enemy.

My companion did not stay in the hutted camp, but travelled back and fore from her farm home nearby. The girls in the camp came from very varied backgrounds; some were country girls, but mostly they came from towns and cities. Whatever their jobs were prior to joining the WTC, they certainly worked very hard and they were always cheerful. Those who worked in the woods alongside the men travelled by lorry to the scene of operations which was about six miles from the camp. I was provided with a man's bicycle. The long journey was by a much pot-holed road in the dark, morning and night, and frequently I was plunged into darkness as the dynamo jumped off the back wheel. At nights, I was always so relieved when I came in sight of the camp lights.

I was there for some time and then I was transferred to a unit where I shared a cottage with three other girls. They were employed on tree planting. The office was about three miles from the cottage and transport was by 'shanks' pony'. I became rather wearied of this and requested a bicycle. A bone-shaker was made up for me by cannibalising other old wrecks. If not altogether elegant it, at least, covered the ground more quickly.

What stands out in my memory most of all was the scarcity of food. Rationing had been introduced by then and we had to subsist on two ounces of this and two ounces of that. I recall that my lunch consisted of two slices of bread and HP sauce. For breakfast we had brose: a handful of oatmeal in a bowl with a pinch of pepper and salt and stirred with boiling water. Along with it, we had a small bowl of milk. The evening meal consisted of a plate of soup and more bread. We did not see very much meat or fish. Probably, however, country people were rather better off than town people because of local produce such as vegetables, occasional eggs and, sometimes, even rabbit. After dinner each night, we had to take turns on the cross-cut saw cutting logs for the fire.

What sort of social life did we have? The short answer is practically none. Village dances in Scotland at that time began about 10.30 pm and lasted until about 3 am. We went to a village dance on one occasion by bicycle, but after we had cycled the eight miles back to camp, it was 5 am and hardly worth going to bed. We just washed, breakfasted and went off to work without even a snooze. Needless to say, we did not repeat that performance.

On another occasion, we stayed in a castle, with the permission of the Factor who knew one of our members quite well. I understand that it was usually occupied by the elderly Laird, but, at that time, he was absent. The Factor gave us his dog to boost our morale in this isolated barracks of a place. One evening, when we were sitting round the fire, the dog suddenly began to growl. Then, he padded stiff-legged to the door. In some trepidation, we opened the door and he ran along the dimly-lit corridor, with us in hot pursuit, down the stairs until he came to the gun room where he stopped, barking and growling. We never discovered what he was chasing as the gunroom door was huge, heavy and well fitting. It was quite an unnerving experience, and we learned later that the room was supposed to be haunted as the result of the butler killing a maid there many years before. It was also said that, sometimes, you could hear a child crying.

There was supposed to be a WTC Newsletter but, all the time I was in the service, I never heard of any local members

receiving a copy. We heard of a Benevolent Fund and I remain curious to know if such a Fund ever existed.

Lack of recognition for our, not inconsiderable, contribution towards the war effort was a sore point and we felt embittered at the end of hostilities to receive a small missive thanking us for our efforts, but no hint of a gratuity or recompense for the destruction of our precious civilian clothing, and no monetary assistance to get back to our various professions. In hairdressing, for example, we had to pay a substantial premium to restart and I, for one, certainly was not able to afford it. So, I just continued in an office.

When this sketchy description of life in the WTC is read, I hope people will realise how much effort the girls put into performing a man's job. When I meet friends from the old days, the bad times are a source of great amusement to us now. Time is a great healer and, looking through photographs, we tend to remember the happier moments and think we would not have missed it all for anything!

SONG OF THE ISLES

This poem is by an ex-WTC member from Stornoway who says that they sang it to the tune of the 'Skye Boat Song'.

When the 'Lochness' sails far over the sea,
Lashed by the wind and the spray,
She'll carry the girls who were felling the trees,
Homeward to Stornoway.

When we're aboard we'll think no more
Of axes we've left behind;
We're going home, never more to roam
Back to the spruce and the pine.

Loved ones are waiting there on the quay,
With hearts that are full of joy,
To welcome the girls who have helped victory,
Along with the gallant boys.

They told us our boys were needed to fight
Far from our native shore;
And who would release them to go to the strife?
The girls who had spirit galore.

And so, one and all, they answered the call
To get into uniform;
Some to the WAAFs and some to the ATS,
But we joined the Timber Corps.

We'll never forget, nor ever regret,
Leaving our island shore;
We wait for the day when we'll be repaid
By peace on earth once more.

JEAN BUNTIN
(NÉE MACNAUGHTON)

Bang! Fizz! It was so cold a bottle of lemonade exploded.

In February 1942, I joined the Women's Forestry Service, the forerunner of the Women's Timber Corps, changing scissors and comb for the much heavier tools of axe and saw. A letter arrived telling me to report to Meiklour camp, near Blairgowrie, taking with me suitable clothing for forestry work. There, a period of training began with Bob Allison teaching us all aspects of timber work: laying-in, felling, snedding, crosscutting, burning the brush and dragging with horse or tractor to the loading points where the pit-props were loaded on to lorries for transfer to the station. We were taught to use four and a half pound axes and cross-cut saws which had to be kept sharp. The largest logs for pit-props measured 14 feet by 8 inch diameter and trees too big for props went to the sawmill where girls also worked. If telegraph poles were required, they were always selected by the District Officer.

Jean Buntin

The weather was very severe for part of that first winter so the thought of the journey to work in the back of an open bogie was not something to make us leap out of bed! Our accommodation was in wooden huts, heated by wood-burning stoves around which we had to dry our wet clothes. It was quite comfortable while the stove was going but the temperature dropped very quickly when the last log burned away. Early one morning I was wakened by a loud bang and a fizzing noise; a bottle of lemonade had exploded with the cold and by breakfast time it had frozen solid! There were no ball point pens then and the ink used to freeze in the bottles in the lockers above our heads. The huts were lit by Tilly lamps which we had to learn to tend. The ablution huts were freezing cold in the winter as the 'windows' in the eaves were unglazed!

We travelled to the woods on the back of a lorry, taking with us our lunch "pieces" and an enamel can of milk for the tea breaks which was often frozen by the time we got there. The work soon warmed us up even though we sometimes had to clear snow away from the trees before felling. The pay was thirty seven shillings a week from which we had to give ten shillings for food and rent and sixpence for clothing.

In April 1942 the Women's Timber Corps was formed and we were issued with a uniform similar to that of the Women's Land Army. Instead of a 'pork-pie' hat there was a green beret and gaberdine in place of corduroy breeches: a khaki shirt, green tie and pullover, a very warm short coat, fawn stockings and brown shoes completed the uniform and for working uniform was dungarees, boots, shirt and oilskins. There were very few days lost through bad weather, although it was very dangerous felling in high winds and very uncomfortable wearing oilskins in the rain.

In late April most of us were moved to Glendoick, a new camp near Kinfauns on the Perth to Dundee road. Paramount News came and filmed us at work in Glendoick and there were even photographs in the New York Times!

Then, in March 1943, I went as a trainer to Shandford Lodge, near Brechin. One hundred and twenty girls arrived at

By this personal message I wish to express to you

J. Macnaughton. W.T.C. 410

my appreciation of your loyal and devoted service
as a member of the Women's Land Army from

22.6.42   to   9.10.45

Your unsparing efforts at a time when the victory
of our cause depended on the utmost use of the
resources of our land have earned for you the
country's gratitude.

Elizabeth R

Shandford every five weeks to be divided among ten trainers who were then responsible for teaching the art of felling, dragging with tractor or horse, loading and driving to the station. At the end of each training session there was a concert before the girls dispersed to camps all over Scotland. They went to Alness, Strachur, Innerleithen, Dumfries, Park House, Alyth, Ethie and to private firms and estates.

After I had been at Shandford for six months I was asked to go to Roughmount as forewoman with Morag Mackenzie as my 'ganger'. We were responsible for the training and welfare of forty-one girls, with the help of a cook, an office-girl and cleaning and kitchen staff. The Food Office was in Forfar, where I went regularly to discuss rations. I remember there was an excellent ration of cheese and each girl had her own pot of jam.

Loading the lorries was a heavy job and, with the driver and her mate, Morag and I would load five tons or more before the lorry was driven to Tannadice station and the pit-props loaded on to wagons. Heavier timber was despatched to Bell and Syme, Dundee, James Donaldson, Tayport, Dorman Long and MacGregor and Balfour. The latter took birch to make pirns for the jute mills.

While at Roughmount I had an alarming experience when the rear wheel of a Fordson tractor came off as I was driving it down Tannadice Brae. Fortunately, the tractor slewed round and a dry stone dyke stopped our descent down a very steep bank.

In 1944 there was great demand for more timber so Morag and I were asked to go to Kinnordy and go on "piece work". The basic wage was two pounds, twelve shillings and six pence and then we were paid tenpence for each tree, felled, snedded, cross-cut into lengths for pit-props and all brush burned. We had the help of an Italian prisoner-of-war for whom we each paid ten shillings per week. Tony was an excellent worker and well worth the money. Before starting the 'piece work' we had a chance to fell a very large sycamore on Glamis estate which we were determined to do ourselves. However, as a seven foot saw had to be used the foreman, Bill

Martin, insisted that we had the help of two German prisoners-of-war. The diameter measured one metre, quite the largest tree I had helped to fell.

It was not all hard work and no play! There was the lorry to take us to Brechin or Forfar on a Wednesday. There were dances in Brechin and we ran our own dances in Glendoick and Roughmount. Often there were Army units stationed nearby which livened up the social scene and, at Kinnordy, ENSA brought films on a regular basis. Among the men of the Royal Signals was a pianist who had played with Henry Hall's Band and we had a piano and also a gramophone which Morag and I had bought for £3 in Dundee, so we were well catered for in the music department.

Little did I think, when I was helping my father to cut firewood when I was still at school that I would work for four years in the woods. Morag and I had been brought up on farms so the transition to the hard life was not quite so difficult for us as it must have been for some city girls, although I had been hairdressing in Glasgow before 1942 and had experienced something of the blitz on the Clyde. We all learned so much from life in the WTC and made lasting friendships.

MOIRA GAFFNEY
(NÉE MCGEE)

What joy to see the daffodils and primroses in the spring.

I joined the Forestry Commission early in 1942 and went to a small camp of six girls at Kells Wood near Southwick in Dumfriesshire. This was in the early days of the war when the Forestry Commission was responsible for Timber Produc-tion, later taken over by the Ministry of Supply Home Grown Timber Production Department. At Kells, we were given a brief training in tree felling, snedding the branches and burning the brushwood, which was very dirty work. From these first tasks we graduated to the portable saw bench where we cross-cut the felled trees into various sizes of pit props. These were stacked in lanes, according to size, ready for uplifting by tractor and trailer or lorry, driven to the station, loaded on to railway wagons and the order con-signed.

Wages amounted to approximately thirty-eight shillings per week on which we had to subsist and purchase our own food. We lived in hutted accommodation and cleaned the huts and cooked by rota. Sanitation was primitive, a dry sump, later upgraded to a chemical toilet, but, horror of horrors, we had to take it in turn to empty the bucket!

By the end of 1942 the Women's Timber Corps was well established and we were kitted out with uniforms. When Kells Wood was finished after a year's hard labour, the six of us were promoted to the rank of Leader and moved on to Newtonairds, seven miles from Dumfries. The camp was designed for twenty girls. We spent nine months there before moving again. Our next move was to Wallaceton, fourteen

Laying In

miles from Dumfries. This camp consisted of four huts with accommodation for ten in each, an ablution hut with showers and hot water (Oh, the luxury!) and a drying area for our washing. All the girls who came to Wallaceton had been previously trained at Shandford near Brechin.

Each morning at 8 am we were transported by lorry to the scene of operations. Lunch time was at noon, when we ate our sandwiches and made tea in a billy can over a fire; work resumed at 12.30 pm and tools were downed at 5.30 pm. In winter, the little robins joined us for lunch and I still love them. We worked half day on Saturdays and had Sundays free. Wallaceton Camp had a Supervisor and full-time Cook who worked wonders with the available food rations.

At every WTC camp in Scotland the members came from all parts of the mainland and from Skye and Mull and the Outer Isles and even Shetland, and from a wide range of backgrounds: some were country girls, others factory and brewery workers, teachers, shop assistants or office girls. I was a clerkess in a large wholesale warehouse in the City of Glasgow. From such environments and relative comfort, we suddenly found ourselves having to adapt to the rough and tumble, the dirt and grime, the wet and the cold of timber operations in a totally different and strange environment. The most testing part was, of course, in winter when the huts were freezing cold with icicles hanging from the ceiling and frost glistening on the walls of the huts in the mornings. Some of the girls purloined their fathers' long johns and slept in them! In the evenings we had the big log stoves well stoked, but they quickly cooled after we went to bed. On reflection, I am sometimes amazed that we were able to carry on working in ice and snow conditions when we could scarcely breathe in the freezing air. Inevitably, there were casualties and a small number who had reached the limits of their endurance had to obtain their release on medical grounds.

Spring, with all its promise, always came round and I recall what joy it was to see the naturalised daffodils and the wild primroses in the woods, the delights of the long summer evenings and then the glory of the autumn colours, followed, all too soon, by dreary winter again. Even then, the snow-capped trees, the purity of the distant hills and the deep stillness of it all was uplifting and remains with me still. We did have some social life to relieve the otherwise fairly drab camp life making as much as possible of our own entertaining talents, but some who had bicycles cycled many miles to country dances. That was a big change from the Palais de Danse and the music of Glen Miller, but we joined in the reels and strathspeys, to fiddle music, with gusto. We sang a lot in camp, putting our own words to the army tunes of the day, and could have been 'Top of the Props'! Evenings were often spent writing letters. On Saturday afternoons we went into town, then off to the Cinema and, sometimes, to the dancing in the YMCA. We tried to get home one weekend every month. Looking back, I think we were a very happy team and dissensions were few.

The war seemed very far away from us until we witnessed an aircraft crashing into the Solway near our first camp and, later, another crashing into the hills around Wallaceton. There was sadness when two of the girls in our hut got news that their boyfriends had been killed on active service. My friend's fiancé had his leg blown off on the day after D-Day and my sister's fiancé was killed in an air crash over Italy. These incidents brought the horrors of war into our peaceful woods.

I recall that the work in the WTC was arduous and that sometimes we were very tired, but we became inured to it and perhaps even thrived on it. It was a wonderful experience in life and a splendid lesson on how to get on with your associates. And the end of it all when the Corps was disbanded – home, no employment, no recognition of what we had achieved for the war effort, no gratuities and no recognition for the WTC. We were truly the Forgotten Corps. Is it any wonder that we felt a little embittered? Still, speaking for myself and my friends, they were the best days of our youth.

ALMORA MURDOCH
(NÉE CRUICKSHANK)

Come quickly, the horse is drowning!

My first land work was as a volunteer to help bring in the harvest in the summer of 1940; as so many men were being called up for military service and the weather was exceptionally fine, the farmers along Deeside were desperate to bring in their crops while the good weather held.

After a short spell of training at Craibstone College of Agriculture, those of us who had by now joined the Land Army proper were deployed among the small farms up and down the rivers Dee and Don. Many had no sanitation, indoor water supply or electricity, and I remember waking at 5.00 am to hear the pump screeching away in the yard outside. It was a forty-eight hour week but many were the times I had to use my bicycle at 11 pm to round up the stirks that had got away, and many were the diatribes I had to listen to anent the local lairds and landlords.

Work on the farm involved the use of Clydesdales, as tractors were very scarce in war time and were mainly on hire, being beyond the means of small farmers at that time. Most farms had at least one pair of horses and I liked these lovely patient beasts, though the wives thought I was brave to go near them at all, so I was quite used to working them when I was asked if I would like to take part in an experiment using girls to help with the dragging of timber in the woods around Aboyne and Coull. We started in the winter of 1941/42 and there was a lot of snow and ice that year. There were four horses and four of us girls, Margaret Strang, the daughter of the gamekeeper at Glentanar, a girl called Jean Haddon, Miss

Timber!

Keiller-Gregg from Ballater, who wasn't with us long, and a girl called Pat, with lovely golden hair.

My first horse was a stubborn old chap called Donald. He really did not want to work at all and was getting past it. We had to shout and, I regret to say, swear at him to get him to move. I was then promoted to a black mare called Katie, who was a delight to get on with, being so intelligent. You just chained up her log and she went off on her own, choosing the best route downhill through the very difficult terrain. The one caterpillar tractor, driven by one of the remaining men, used to gather and stack the logs, but it was always getting stuck in the mud. We played some awful tricks on these older men. At one point, in the middle of really icy weather, we pretended that Katie had fallen into the burn. It was April 1st, but still very wintry! We hid her, then rushed screaming up to the chap on the tractor, saying 'Come quickly, the horse is drowning!' He was furious when he found us out! We never did that sort of thing again. But one day there was another screeching and yelling. This was Pat of the golden hair being held down by the men to see if they could check if her hair colour was real!

Sometimes there were accidents. One day a tree fell on one of the men and broke his back. We watched him being stretchered out of the woods, never to return. But I think he survived. The men were constantly being sought by the Labour Exchange 'mannie' whose job it was to check on the evaders from the call-up.

We were paid top wages of £2.5/- per week; in the Land Army it was 30/-. Sometimes you got your keep as well, if living in at the farm. Our uniform was provided; a green wool pullover, cord breeches, stockings, gumboots, dungarees and a couple of white shirts to wear under them. We also had a hat and strong shoes for smarter wear. I reckoned that we walked about fifteen miles in a day.

The logs we dragged were mainly fir and pine for pit props and old birch for bobbins in clothes factories. I felt this was hardly war work, but no doubt the bobbins were important to someone. The logs had already been cut and trimmed by the older men, all done by hand-saw.

Almora Murdoch

After about seven months I had a chance through a friend to join a slightly more advanced type of war work, calculating cubic dimensions of standing timber for the Forestry Commission under Sir Henry Beresford Pierce. But I was not allowed to leave the Land Army, so I went on to work in the gardens of Glentaner House where I stayed until my marriage in 1943, in the chapel of the Glentaner Estate.

The Women's Timber Corps proved to be a great success in spite of the gloomy predictions of some people. I was very happy in the outdoors and was glad to have helped to show that girls could also work in the woods.

THE NATION'S LARDER NEEDS REFILLING!

Or so it will from mid-August to the end of September when Scotland's huge crops of grain will have ripened.

The reaper will move in among these crops, but who will gather the sheaves?

For that vital job Scotland needs 12,000 fit and willing volunteers—willing to spend a week or more in the open-air staying at a harvest hostel and helping Scotland out of an emergency on the Home Front.

Fill in the attached coupon for details of wages, transport facilities, etc.

HELP WITH THE HARVEST

NAME,............................

ADDRESS,........................

....

CUT OUT AND POST TO

THE DEPARTMENT OF AGRICULTURE FOR SCOTLAND, 15 GROSVENOR STREET, EDINBURGH, 12.   G 17

45

WILMA MCLULLICH
(NÉE MUIR)

It was a happy, healthy life in the open air.

When I enrolled for wartime service, I actually applied for the WAAFS but failed the medical test. I was then instructed to enrol for Munitions or the NAAFI but medical advice was that I must have work in the open air.

I had a friend in the Women's Timber Corps who suggested that I should report to the Ministry of Supply Office and volunteer for work in the woods. Acceptance was immediate and no further medical was required. I was instructed to travel to the Training Centre at Shandford Lodge and report to Mr Bob Allison who was the Chief Instructor. I spent a month there under the tuition of a WTC leader who had been trained by Bob Allison.

My first job after leaving Shandford was with Bryant and May, the match firm, at Sandbank near Dunoon (Balloch Estate) thinning a Sitka Spruce wood for making matches. I recall the awful time we had with midgies which nearly drove us crazy. We were a WTC gang of eight. Bryant and May very generously gave us a box of matches every second week, but we had to pay for them. They were saved up and taken home and gladly received because matches were in scarce supply. We worked there for six months, then moved to lovely Glendaruel for a year, where we were engaged in stacking pit props in rows according to top diameter. It was all very hard work but we became inured to that as we grew fitter. Twelve of us lived in the basement of Glendaruel Lodge.

I was then sent down to Loch Striven for six weeks and worked as an orderly at Inverchaolain House and then had a big transfer from Argyllshire to Wallaceton near Moniaive in Dumfriesshire where we were engaged in felling oak and conifers for eighteen months, loading lorries and unloading into wagons at the station. I occasionally went to New-tonairds to see a friend and stayed in the camp there with her.

Wallaceton Camp closed down on VE Day when I moved back to Argyllshire and stayed at Letters Lodge for six weeks, working on the sawbench. Then on 7th December 1945 we were disbanded.

I had no trouble about uniform, being kitted out immedi-ately after completing my training at Shandford. All trainees at Shandford were similarly treated on completing the course. Elsewhere, others were less fortunate and wore out their own clothing before receiving their uniforms. They received neither compensation nor even extra clothing coupons, which was a great injustice. We were allowed two weeks' holiday a year but had to work half day on Saturdays. Pay was very meagre.

On reflection, in spite of all the hard work and drudgery, it was a happy, healthy life in the open air and the splendid camaraderie and lasting friendships are recalled with happi-ness. This is enhanced annually by a reunion of old friends at Ballachulish, meeting sometimes for a weekend and reminis-cing happily about those splendid days. Although our num-bers have been depleted by one or two who have passed away, my companions now are: Betty Hunter (née Inglis), Sheila Bain (née McKinnon), Sandra Baxter, Margaret MacDonald, Alice Taylor, Mary Blue (née Shaw), Janet McLarty, Jessie MacDonald and Mary McKinnon.

JEAN SMITH
(NÉE LUMSDEN)

We drew water from a well in a white enamel bucket.

I was only nineteen when my call-up papers arrived in 1941 and, as I had been working as a clerkess after leaving school, I was lucky to be taken on in a similar position at Shandford Lodge with the Women's Timber Corps. My job there was to explain to new girls in the office about how to organise the timber consignments to the station and all the associated paper work. I had a Morris 8 with a soft top, supplied by the Ministry of Supply, and drove to Forfar station to consign the timber. The smallest logs measured two and a half feet by two and a half inch diameter and the largest sixteen feet by nine inches. They were huge logs to manhandle. Fortunately I never had to do service in the woods! How the girls managed it, I do not know.

I worked for a time in Leven, in Fife, and remember collecting the money to pay the men from the Star Hotel on Friday mornings and when I went back to get the money to pay the women in the afternoon, I received the same notes over again. The men had been celebrating pay day!

With another girl, I spent some time at a camp in Struan, Perthshire. There we lived in a small cottage away from the men's huts. If the tap refused to produce water we had to go to a well and draw up water in a white enamel bucket. It was all quite an experience! There were prisoners-of-war working in the woods there, sometimes Germans, sometimes Austrians and sometimes Italians. They were always very polite to the office girls.

On the last day of the war, I heard that my husband had

been killed on active service in Germany so, afterwards, when we were given the opportunity to go to Germany, I decided to try that. The Control Commission required girls, familiar with timber work, to do secretarial work in the North German Timber Control.

There was a big detachment near Brunswick, the nearest town to the Russian zone, to which I was posted. I also was in Hanover, Hamburg and a lovely place called Wolfsburg, where the Volkswagen Beetles were made. It was my favourite place.

There was no antagonism in the offices in which I worked. In Brunswick the woman in charge of the office was a German who was extremely efficient and had an excellent grasp of languages. With my experience of consigning loads of timber in Scotland, I was often given that task in Germany. We tried to see as much of the country as possible and the devastation was terrible in cities such as Hamburg.

One thing which pleased us was to find a dressmaker who ran up skirts and dresses for social occasions. We had been issued with some clothing by the Control Commission: a blue suit, two pairs of black stockings, a greatcoat, one pair of black shoes, two shirts, four collars, a cap, shoulder titles, a black tie and a cap badge.

When I decided to go to Germany, I signed up for one year only but, in the end, stayed for three years. It helped me to get over the loss of my husband.

I still keep my WTC beret and badge and meet up with friends from those far off days.

SANDRA MANSON
(NÉE BAXTER)

The next question was 'Can you swim?'

When I was called up in 1942 I joined the Women's Timber Corps and was sent for five weeks' training to Glen Etive. There, we were taught all aspects of forestry; laying-in, felling, cross-cutting, snedding and loading on to lorries for transportation to the nearest station, where the load would be consigned for transfer by rail.

The work was hard for girls, but we enjoyed the companionship and made the best of conditions which were far from luxurious at times.

In May 1944, I was posted to Elderslie to work in the office there. The job only lasted for four weeks before I was given an order to board the train to Dalmally. No explanation was given! Mr Dow, the forester, met me at the station and we proceeded to Ardbrecknish Manse, where the Timber Corps girls were billeted. During the course of our journey he persisted in asking me about my experience of boats to which I could only reply that it was very little. The next question was 'Can you swim?' I said that I could, but still no explanation was given for these strange questions!

Instead of going to the billet, we went straight to the jetty, bag and baggage, where I met the travelling mechanic from Alexandria. He was working on an ex-Navy liberty boat which required a new clutch. So, Donny, the mechanic, and I spent an exhausting day fitting the new clutch. I had no mechanical experience before I started but just followed instructions and, by the end of the day, we were in business again! Donny took me out to show me how to operate the engine and then left me to get on with it. I felt very proud that first evening when I took the men up Loch Awe without mishap.

On the steep sides of the lochs it was easier to extract the logs by forming a 'raft' and towing them along the loch from a 'rafting bay' to a suitable loading point where they were transferred to a lorry for transport to the station.

I remember it was a glorious summer morning when we started 'rafting', with the loch like a sheet of glass but, in spite of such favourable conditions, I felt quite apprehensive about the day of rafting which lay ahead. Would I be able to manage? However, as I set off for the rafting bay I felt my confidence return.

Horses dragged the timber to the water's edge where two WTC members, complete with waders, were waiting to unchain the logs. One girl then floated the logs and held them in position, while the other fastened them together with 'dogs', metal rings with sharp spikes sticking out of them, placed at intervals along a chain, and hammered firmly into the butt-end of the trees. A strong rope was then tied to the centre log of the raft and the other end passed to me on the boat. This end was secured to an iron hook, fitted in the stern, and then I was ready to set off with my raft.

On safe arrival at my destination, I was met by another WTC girl who waded out as far as possible to catch the rope which I unhooked and threw to her. I then turned the boat out of the way of the incoming logs and the girl drew them in to the beach. This process was repeated and, as long as the weather remained good, it was relatively easy. On a fine day, about two hundred trees were extracted by this method.

As we were rafting at the narrowest point of Loch Awe, it could be quite stormy and, in a strong wind, we had to abandon rafting but only once was I caught in the middle of the loch, quite unable to make headway. I was blown off course, drifting in the mist, to the opposite end of the loch, so I cut the engine and tried to steer nearer the shore. It was with relief that I caught sight of the old pier so I made for it to obtain some shelter, remaining there till I felt it was safe to go and collect the workers.

My experience of rafting was both interesting and enjoyable and made a change from working in the woods.

I still keep in touch with friends from these war years when we meet annually. The 'Girls of Etive' were very close companions, both then and now.

ELIZABETH HUNTER
(NÉE BETTY INGLIS)

The 'Girls of Etive' were always close friends and, for some of their reunions, Elizabeth Hunter (née Betty Inglis) composed these poems.

GIRLS OF ETIVE

1987

When the Timber Corps was formed in 1942
Country girls and town girls started life anew;
None, I am sure, will ever forget that journey from
    Tyndrum Station
Across the moors to Glenetive road end, where stood
    our transportation;
A great big dirty lorry, Geordie Maxwell at the wheel
He told us all to scramble on, we thought, 'God, this
    can't be real!';
For miles along a bumpy road we were tossed about
    that lorry
When at last we reached Glenetive House, not one of
    us was sorry.
We were led into the kitchen, given tea – but not in
    a cup
It was served in enormous thick white mugs that
    need both hands to pick up;
We didn't get much of a welcome, Mrs Fisher,
    glowering from left to right
Sneeringly remarking, 'To me, you are just ships that
    pass in the night';

Timber!

We soon knew how it felt to go hungry, we got used
to eating stale bread
Kept mouldy in drawers and gnawed at by rats,
whose presence we really did dread.
When Mrs Fisher was shown the road, we were in
for a pleasant surprise
Miss Robertson arrived to take over, an angel in
disguise;
We christened her 'wee Fanny', no disrespect was
meant
'Cause each and every one of us believed her heaven
sent;
Her feeding gave us stamina for the work we had to
do
Jobs we never thought we'd tackle – we were a
motley crew;
We were taught to fell and sned a tree, lay in and
burn the brush
Load lorries, tractors, boats and trains – they made
good use of us.
We dug ditches with picks and shovels, made the
'Burma Road' with slabs
Filling it in with sawdust, here and there in dribs and
drabs;
We had blistered hands and backache, worked like
'drookit craws' in rain
And the midgies did their level best to drive us all
insane;
We lost our 'wellies' in the muck, our eyes streamed
with the smoke
Trapped our fingers at the saw-bench and dodging
dislodged boulders was no joke.
Some may think we should forget the torture we
went through
But it's nice to meet and laugh at the things we used
to do;
So here's to the 'Girls of Etive' who in wartime acted
as men

Elizabeth Hunter

Good Luck, Good Health and God bless You,
TRUE MONARCHS OF THE GLEN.

MORE ABOUT THE GIRLS OF ETIVE

1989

Now that I've reminded you of our introduction to
   the Glen
Cast your mind back to those timber days, while I
   reminisce again;
The camp was put on production and we were the
   chosen few
Kept on to greet new arrivals and show them what
   to do.
Our blistered hands now calloused, we had
   developed stronger backs
And muscles formed on our arms, through swinging
   a seven pound axe;
Ours was the most isolated camp of all, just
   mountains roamed by deer
But we used to tell the new girls, 'There's a picture-
   house down at the pier!!!';
Remember the big long dining hall, antlers overhead
Where we used to argue whose turn it was to go up
   and ask for more bread;
You were ambushed when you left the hatch, like
   fish grabbing at the bait
By the time you reached the dining-hall, you held an
   empty plate!
We were thirty girls with two bathrooms, privacy
   just wasn't known
There would be a girl in the bath, a girl at the sink
   and another one sat on the throne;
And standing outside would be two or three more,
   chuntering and making a song
Knocking the door, shouting 'Who's that in there,

what are you doing?' and 'Are you going to be
long?'
As time went by we were privileged to use the
sitting-room downstairs
And two adjacent toilets – an answer to our prayers;
We held 'At Homes' in the sitting-room, playing
games and singing and dancing
And some of the girls who had boyfriends, even
found time for romancing
I think of Mima when I hear 'Ramona'; Terry sang
'The Old House' and a lot more
'Smoke gets in your Eyes' sung by Sheila and you'll
remember Dan the Darkie's 'Stardust', I'm sure;
We could spend the night reminiscing but, by me,
enough has been said
So here's hoping we have lots more reunions in the
years that are lying ahead.

'PIECE' TIME

1995

Over fifty years ago, we all were in our prime
But now our faces and bodies show the ravages of
time;
Once we swung a mighty axe and pulled a cross-cut
saw
But we couldn't fell a tree now, without stopping for
a 'blaw'.
We're short of breath, our joints are stiff and we
moan of aches and pain
But when reunion time comes round, we'll feel young
again;
Our worries all are put aside, as we start to reminisce
Remember this, remember that and who remembers
this?

Elizabeth Hunter

Our 'pieces' for our mid-day snack, made up of
cheese and jam
Sometimes we had banana spread, sometimes it was
spam;
The jam was made of vegetables, with flavouring
and coloured,
Banana spread was flavoured parsnips we discovered!
When break-time came we raked the fire and placed
our billy-cans
A forked branch was used to toast our bread – my,
it tasted grand!
Sometimes our bread fell in the fire, we'd give a little
curse
Then fish it out and blow on it and scrape away the
dust.
We drank straight from our billy-cans, our hands
were never clean
No time to think of hygiene, or where our hands had
been;
We looked like bloomin' tinkers, squatting round the
fire
A tougher, rougher bunch of girls, but with guts to
be admired
When asked how we coped with the elements, hard
work and midgies as well
Our answer in a nutshell, 'IT WAS ABSOLUTELY
HELL.'

KATIE ANN KENNEDY
(NÉE MACKENZIE)

They were even given working gloves!

As I had not reached 'calling-up' age I volunteered to go with my school friend to work in forestry at Corriemony, Glenurquhart. When we came from Skye in 1940, it was my first time on the mainland. We stayed in a youth hostel until the huts were built. It was over a year before we had uniforms, inferior to the those worn by the Canadian Forestry Corps, which was a measure of our wartime restrictions. They were even given working gloves! I remember our reconditioned wellington boots leaking and our black boots resembling cardboard when they got wet. We started off peeling pit-props, then graduated to felling trees. Two of us on piece-work could fell one hundred trees a day, snedding and sawing them into mill wood, pit-props and pulp. We were paid one shilling for each tree. It proved to be too hard for girls.

After that we were given a horse each for hauling wood to a point where the tractor could collect it. We loved the horses who became our firm friends. The work also included loading railway trucks with pit props and pulp wood, working at the saw mill and making roads for tractors with slabs and saw-dust.

When the work at Corriemony was finished we moved to Contin where we stayed in Craigdarroch Lodge which is now a hotel. There, we had a cook and supervisor to look after us. Our boss in the woods was Dan Sutherland.

The weekends were eagerly anticipated when we used to run our own dances in Contin Hall which had bare floors,

Rain, hail or shine

shutters instead of curtains and was very cold. We slept in Army beds and had to fold them, Army style, every morning.

We managed to raise enough cash to buy a sewing machine, which was very useful as clothes were so scarce. Our clothing coupons were used for working clothes until we were issued with uniform, so we didn't have any for buying smart clothes. We went to Dingwall or Inverness on Saturdays, had lovely fish and chips and ice-cream and then went to the 'pictures'.

We were very healthy and happy, out in all weathers, working in the snow and frost and, of course, in glorious sunshine, well away from the horrors of the war.

I still write to some of my friends after over fifty years. We were very close, more like sisters.

Austerity in women's clothing

Austerity in clothing affected all women in the country. Members of the WTC dressed up for their dances and social evenings and had to 'make do and mend' with the rest!

Orders were made in May 1942 banning fur and all trimmings on outdoor clothing and prohibiting the use of lace and embroidery from June 1942 on manufactured nightwear.

There should be no extras on coats such as flares, capes, braid and embroidery, applique and quilting. No fur, velvet, silk, rayon or leather trimmings should be used and buttonholes for decorative purposes would not be allowed.

Skirts should not have more than three buttons, six seams, one pocket, two inverted pleats or four knife pleats. No skirt should have accordion pleating, leather, fur or velvet trimming.

No adult garment should have a hem exceeding one inch but there would be an exception for children's garments not subject to purchase tax.

However, the Board of Trade declared that there was nothing to stop women making their own underclothes and embroidering them! One group of WTC bought a sewing machine to help with the clothing problem.

Katie Ann Kennedy

Go through
your wardrobe

Make-do
and Mend

Timber!

New standardised sizes of women's dresses would soon be introduced, said the Board of Trade, the object of which was to give good value for clothing coupons and reduce the tedious business of trying-on clothes in shops. A new mail order scheme was soon to be introduced. There would be **thirty-six** new sizes! A,B,C,D, . . . with A1 denoting a large hip size, A2, a large bust size and so on! Where are all these sizes today?

Men did not escape either. Shirt tails were to be shorter, there would be fewer buttons, no pockets and no double cuffs. Pyjamas would have no pockets or embroidery and not more than three buttons.

MARTHA L GRANT
(NÉE BROWNLIE)

Census work could be very frustrating!

I am over eighty years old now and have always felt that my medal for the war years was the badge that I still possess. It is inscribed 'Women's Forestry Service – Home Timber Supplies', as it was known in the Borders before being seconded to the Ministry of Supply.

I knew the valuable and heavy work that was carried out by city and local girls in a cheerful and uncomplaining manner because I was in charge of a unit of thirty-six girls at Rutherford, near Kelso, for four years. Afterwards, I was involved in forestry census work.

Census work could be very frustrating. A flying census had been taken in Scotland in 1941 of woods over five acres but now all the green patches on our map had to be visited and surveyed, giving a rough idea of the volume of timber there. Sometimes we would walk for hours only to find that the trees were either useless for our purpose or had already been felled!

In a wood the sampling method was used. We measured each tree in a tenth of an acre by taking the girth and estimating the height. The volume of timber could then be calculated and if it was suitable for pit props or telegraph poles the Acquisition Officer would then contact the owner and offer a price for his timber.

The census work took us all over the countryside and, while it sounded complicated to the uninitiated, we enjoyed the challenge of working with figures.

As I have always felt that the Women's Timber Corps was

Timber!

treated as a poor relation of the Women's Land Army, I hope that, after reading these stories, people will be more aware of the splendid work carried out by the girls of the Timber Corps.

MARY RALPH
(NÉE MITCHELL)

I replied to Her Majesty that we wore dungarees in the wood.

I was called up on 23rd July 1942 and started my timber work with the Forestry Commission at Garmouth, near Lossie-mouth. My companions were all local girls. The first job was peeling the trees; then our boss, Mr McLean, started four of us on felling with a quick lesson and then left us to it. One day, just after we had started, the boss came to me and said, 'Were you visiting your relations on the other side of the woods last night, Mary?' I said that I had been over and he asked if I had seen any beavers. Of course there were no beavers in our woods, so I just looked puzzled until he explained that something had certainly been gnawing at the trees! As you can imagine, we made a mess of it at first but soon got into the way of it, although we were never allowed near the big saws.

Then I was picked to go as a trainer to Shandford Lodge. We were there for a month before the girls arrived for training from Mr. Allison. We learned so much from him and respected his great knowledge of trees. I am in touch with him still.

When the new recruits arrived, fifty of them for a start, the real job started. We were very sorry for them, coming out of offices, shops and other indoor jobs to such a hard life. However, they adapted quickly, making lasting friendships. The country girls learned to use the axe and saw easily, having been brought up with such things, but the town girls found it very hard. I remember my father teaching me to use a cross-cut saw when I was quite young. The girls learned to cut pit-props: felling, snedding, cutting the timber into lengths and then loading the logs on to the lorry to be taken to the station.

From Shandford I went to Park House, Aberdeenshire, the home of the late Sir Robert and Lady Williams which had been taken over as a training centre, similar to Shandford Lodge. Physical training was a feature of daily life at Park, designed to develop the muscles. There I learned the art of measuring in order to assess the output of timber in a unit. This called for care and accuracy but no advanced mathematics!

My next move was to Dunphail in Morayshire where I was in charge of a unit of WTC girls for a spell. Jim Hendry was our boss in the woods and, like Bob Allison, insisted on things being done correctly. Careless work in the woods could lead to nasty accidents. The key word when felling was '**Timber!**', giving those nearby time to move away from the falling tree.

After Dunphail I went to Dumfries as a measurer, converting trees into cubic feet! Crathie was my next posting where I was also in charge of a group of girls.

Some of the WTC girls sang in the choir in Crathie church. At a sale of work for the church we were requested to turn up in uniform as the Queen, Princess Elizabeth and Princess Margaret Rose were to be there and had asked to meet us. A photograph of the Queen speaking to me appeared in the local newspaper. She was very smart, wearing a lovely hat with a little veil and a dress and coat to match. The Princesses wore their favourite tweed jackets and kilts. The Queen talked to each of us in turn, asking me where we worked. When I told her we had been mainly in Ballochbuie forest, she said they knew it well. They all seemed so interested in our work. It was a very warm day so we were carrying our overcoats on our arms and Her Majesty asked if we had light, suitable clothing for the heavy outdoor work we did? I replied that we wore dungarees! It was an honour for us to have spoken to the Queen for so long. After that we had another visit from Her Majesty and her daughters while we worked in the woods at Invercauld. They just appeared one day with Mr

Farquhar from Invercauld and again asked a lot of questions and seemed very impressed with our arduous life in the forest. It really made us feel that we were doing something worthwhile for the war effort.

'**Lumberjills Show Skill and Stamina**', a headline in the Aberdeen '*Press and Journal*' proclaimed in August 1944. 'North-east lumberjills showed Aberdeen holidaymakers how women are tackling a wartime job. Spectators cheered and the traditional woodman's cry of '**Timber!**' resounded through Hazelhead woods amid the crash of falling trees as the girls staged a demonstration of their work following a parade of some 130 girls of the Women's Timber Corps. 'But for you the country and the fighting forces would have been much, much worse off' was the tribute paid to the girls by Sir Thomas Mitchell when he presented two-year service badges after the demonstration. At least, some people appreciated us then!

It was great while it lasted and I made such a lot of friends with whom I still keep in touch, though they are scattered all over this country and abroad.

I received the following poem from my friend Molly Hogg to revive old memories after we left the Timber Corps. I've kept it all these years and still meet up with Molly from time to time to reminisce.

Memories from Afar

Mary, oh Mary, can *you* tell *me*,
How the Timber Corps will flourish without you and me.
Without us wee lassies at its beck and call,
I'm waiting each day for its downfall.

The good old Corps, we'll ne'er forget.
The happy memories of the folk we met,
Of Shandford Lodge and Brechin Toon,
And the pranks we played by the licht o' the moon.

Of midnight parties, of concerts and fun,
In memory we'll recall each one.
When asked what we did in the second Great War,
We'll proudly say '**We were in the Timber Corps**'.

But, Mary Mitchell, I'll ne'er forget,
Though in my corner, old and bent,
I'll aye remember you, my friend,
And work and play and letters penned.

Molly Hogg

ROSE SIMPSON
(NÉE SIMPSON)

Even my dad's long johns were cut down to size!

I was a lumberjill for four years. Being small for my age when I was eighteen, I was unable to join any of the Military Services so I volunteered for the Women's Forestry Service, as it was known before 1942.

First of all, I was sent to Bamff Estate, three miles from Alyth where I lived in a hut with a group of other girls. It was very cold when winter set in and at that time we had to provide our own clothing. When we complained to the Forestry Commission they gave us short leather boots, wellington boots and a yellow raincoat with a sou'wester. If it rained we all looked like Captain Bird's Eye! I was lucky. As my four brothers were away doing their service, I pinched their socks, jumpers, trousers, jackets and even my dad's long johns were cut down to size! Still we complained about wanting a "walking out" uniform, so we were given a green drill suit along with a badge to sew on to the pocket. The badge was inscribed with WFS – Women's Forestry Service.

In 1942 the Women's Timber Corps was formed and we were then given a uniform similar to that of the Land Army though the headgear was different. We wore a beret with a badge with a fir tree motif instead of a round hat with a sheaf of corn.

I remember practising for a parade in Dundee. For three weeks a sergeant from the Highland Infantry, stationed at Alyth, taught us to march in time. On the big day, we marched from Riverside Drive right through the town, escorted by the Dundee City Pipe Band, to the City Square where Sir Garnet Wilson, the Lord Provost, presented us with long service badges which we later sewed on to our great-coats. We then marched to Kidd's Rooms in Lindsay Street where we had pie, cakes, biscuits and tea. It was a great day for us. At last, we thought recognition was being made for our service to our country at war.

One winter, when it became unbearably cold, we exchanged our freezing huts for the much superior accommodation of a mansion house on the estate which belonged to Lord and Lady Ramsay, relatives of the Queen Mother's family at Glamis.

When we finished felling and clearing on Bamff Estate, we all moved to Roughmount camp, Fern, near Brechin, where we stayed in huts. Sometimes we would go to Brechin by lorry to the library and the cinema and occasionally to Forfar to a dance. At a dance in Alyth I met my husband, who was in the Royal Artillery. After his posting to Burma, we corresponded for three years before being married on his return home at the end of the war. In January, 1997 we celebrated our fiftieth wedding anniversary.

Unfortunately, I had to leave Roughmount before the war finished as my mother became ill and I still had two younger sisters at school who required care at home. I had to attend a tribunal in Dundee to apply for compassionate leave. My only regret about leaving early is that I did not receive a certificate of thanks from the Queen.

I loved the work and the grand company of the girls and still keep in touch with Jean 'Stevie' Robertson and Rose Millar. We all greatly enjoyed the reunions in Perth in 1990, 1991 and 1992. It was quite a challenge identifying the 'girls' after so many years!

BETTY PIGGOT
(NÉE CROLL)

I wanted to go into the WRNS!

At the outbreak of war I was in a reserved occupation, working in the office of the North British Rubber Company. When Singapore fell, our work came to an end and we were eligible to be called up. I wanted to go into the WRNS but all I was offered was Munitions or the Land Army. Munitions seemed noisy and I didn't like cows, so the newly formed Women's Timber Corps was suggested as an alternative. A love of trees made this an attractive option.

Before long, I was on my way to the Glen, Innerleithen, where I became WTC member No 33. And so began a life which was often hard but which also had many enjoyable moments. When you are young you forget the hardships quickly.

Later, I was transferred to Shandford Lodge to become a trainer with Bob Allison. Life there was very enjoyable and I made many lasting friendships. Everyone called me 'Crolly'!

My mother then became ill so I was lucky to get a posting to a sawmill in Edinburgh, enabling me to live at home.

I look back on my days in the WTC with happy memories and still meet up with friends to reminisce.

DEIRDRE MACKENZIE
(NÉE MACPHERSON)

They were either too young or too old . . . !

To avoid being sent south to a munitions factory, I joined the newly formed Women's Timber Corps in 1942. After the relative comfort of home, living in wooden huts was quite a shock to the system. In winter, the most desirable position for your bed was beside the wood-burning stove! Sometimes, it was so cold in Speyside that a hot water bottle, fallen out of a narrow bed during the night, would be solid in the morning. We also had to be careful with the ink bottles in our lockers. If they froze and cracked, there would be wailing from the owner of a new dress when the thaw came! But, on days of extreme cold when crystals sparkled in the air and our noses froze up, it was a joy to see the countryside clothed in a blanket of snow.

Although often late in arriving, spring and summer in the woods were delightful times. The abundance of wildlife and plants interested me greatly. Some of the older men were very knowledgeable and taught the girls a great deal about birds and wild flowers. Since then, I have retained an abiding interest in nature. The sound of the first cuckoo never fails to thrill!

The squirrels objected strongly to their habitat being destroyed. It was sad to see their nests, dreys, in felled trees. I often wished I owned a camera in those days. The opportunities for interesting photographs were many, though, sometimes, we were too tired to notice! Now, I never travel without my camera. When I married and went to live in Canada, I took a course in photography and have had many pictures published in magazines but my own favourites are those taken in Speyside on visits home to Scotland.

It was a hard life in the woods, doing the work of men, but we seemed to thrive on it; often tired and hungry, but glowing with good health. Most of the timber we felled was used for pit props in the mines but, as the trees grew tall and straight in Speyside, telegraph poles were also produced. Selecting the trees for poles was a job I enjoyed. Before a wood was felled, suitable trees were ringed with white paint so that they would not be sawn up after felling. We used to buy up all the white paint in Aviemore, Carrbridge and Kingussie! There was something very exciting about the moment when a tree was ready to fall; the cry of **'Timber!'**, followed by the swish and thud of branches hitting the ground. Thirty, forty, fifty years of growth felled in five minutes.

Before timber can be felled, permission has to be sought from the landowner. This process is called 'Acquisition' and requires a great deal of tact on the part of the Acquisition Officer. There was one estate owner near Newtonmore who was very reluctant to part with his beloved trees. Mr Macpherson, Glentruim, could not understand why we would want to convert his woods into pit props but, of course, had to agree in the end. I remember him walking around his trees saying a last goodbye to them. It was very hard for him. The landowners were paid for the timber according to volume-one of the calculations the measurers had to perform.

There were several forest fires in the Glenmore area and I remember the men coming home, faces like coal miners and quite exhausted, after fighting a fire for days. If the ground was peaty, the fire would go underground and be very difficult to control. It could burn for weeks, smouldering under ground and breaking out occasionally. Speedy action was extremely important in reporting and extinguishing these fires, as whole woods could be destroyed in a very short time in dry summer months.

Rationing meant that food was fairly monotonous but, being always so hungry, we really did not mind as long as the diet was reasonable. I think we were lucky in Speyside,

Tea Break

compared to some other places. Our cook was pretty good at acquiring rabbit for a nourishing stew and, occasionally, we even had venison, with no questions asked! At lunchtime we ate sandwiches in the wood and made tea in a billy can over a fire. If the firewood was wet, we would pour on a little diesel to help it along: quite against the rules and producing foul fumes! The lack of fresh fruit in the winter months did not really seem to affect us, although we sometimes longed for a juicy orange. Even marmalade was scarce as oranges became less available. Some girls talked about bananas, but I could not remember ever seeing one!

The Canadians were astonished at our relatively small, unsafe sawmills, machines and lack of lifting gear. Unlike the Newfoundlanders, they came supplied with their own equipment: TD 9 caterpillars, sulkies with huge pneumatic tyres and rotary sawmills which used 'dogs', metal hooks with spikes, to hold the logs, so that, unlike us, they were less liable to lose fingers! Their winches were huge compared to ours but, of course, so were the trees they were designed to lift! With both Canadians and 'Newfies' in the area, Speyside became one of the busiest parts of the country in the production of timber. The stations at Aviemore, Carrbridge and Kingussie were bustling places in those war years.

Social life was good, with camps of 'Newfies' and the Canadian Forestry Corps in the vicinity providing us with entertainment. We went to dances, concerts and whist drives at the weekends and it was at a dance that I met my husband, a Canadian lumberjack. These young men, in their checked lumber jerkins, were like a breath of fresh air to us with all our own boys away in war service. The men who remained were, according to the song we sang, '. . . either too young or too old, They're either too grey or too grassy green . . .' It was no unusual sight to see lumberjacks pedalling off to a dance with a girl perched on the handlebars of the bicycle! It all seemed very exciting and remote from the war.

After the war, we went to live near Vancouver, in the state of British Columbia in Canada, where we have lived ever since, loving the sense of space in this huge country of tall trees, high mountains and hospitable people. However, I still retain happy memories of my years in the Scottish Women's Timber Corps and, when we return to Scotland every second year, we always revisit the sites in Speyside where we worked and met during the war and enjoy visits to reminisce with old friends.

JAMES ROBERTSON AND SONS (P.M.) LTD.
Golden Shred Works - London - Paisley - Manchester - Bristol

'We could do with thousands more like you..'

JOIN THE
WOMEN'S LAND ARMY

Apply to NEAREST W·L·A COUNTY OFFICE or to W·L·A HEADQUARTERS 6, CHESHAM STREET, LONDON S.W.I

Issued by the Ministry of Labour and National Service in conjunction with the Ministry of Agriculture

ALISON MCLURE

A neatly cut V – but you would think a mouse had done it!

1942 was a dark year for Great Britain. The Battle of Britain was over but U-boats were busy targeting our ships, both merchant and navy. It was time for me to volunteer for service.

'There are no vacancies in the Land Army but a new section called the Women's Timber Corps is being started up. I would go myself if I were younger,' sighed my employer, reporting on recruiting information to me. 'They have picnics in the woods every day!' It sounded good so I decided to go for it.

Departure day dawned and bright sunshine lit up Edinburgh Castle as a group of us sped along Princes Street in a tramcar towards the Caledonian Station and the train which would take us to Forfar for the start of our training. We grew more and more silent as our destination approached and during the short bus journey to Brechin we wondered what lay ahead. Then our home for the next four weeks was in front of us, Shandford Lodge.

The first weekend was spent inside; being measured for a uniform, receiving some of the items, having a medical and then drinking tea out of massive mugs. Gone was the delicate china of pre-war years! On Sunday evening we were asked to congregate in the beautiful ballroom of the Lodge to get to know each other. I wish now that I had been able to appreciate the setting more, though I do remember the lovely parquet floor. The Commandant asked for volunteers to play the piano to start a sing-song. Not a movement! So, with my heart in my mouth, I slowly got to my feet and walked to the piano in the corner. It was a great success and everyone joined in the popular songs of the day with great gusto. That was the first of many happy evenings.

On Monday morning we had to break the ice from the outside tap before getting water to wash. Then we did envy the girls who stayed in the Lodge itself! Many of us lived in huts in the grounds. Believe me, it was a 'cat's wash' that first morning: hands, face and neck, all at break-neck speed, back in to finish dressing and then over to the big house for a breakfast of porridge and the inevitable huge mug of tea. Then on went our boots and we paraded in our working clothes to answer to our names before marching off like the seven dwarfs to see the 'wood face' for the first time. The sun shone again and the walk of a mile and a half was enjoyable. We were then handed our axes, shown what to do and left to practise handling them before being introduced to all the other aspects of forest work: felling, snedding and using the tricky double handled saw. The trees were cut very near ground level, not as you see them today with two foot stumps. At the end of a month we had a test and this was my result: 'A neatly cut V, but you would think a mouse had done it.' As I viewed the chips at the foot of the tree, I had to agree! I had worked in an office till then and had had no time to build up my muscles.

When we went into town on our first Saturday outing we wore full dress uniform: green beret, greatcoat, green jumper, breeches of officers' material, knee length socks and very good brown shoes. Very smart!

One Saturday afternoon there was a terrific noise coming from a hut and, upon investigating, I found girls perched on windowsills, beds and lockers screaming their heads off. The cause? A fast moving mouse!

By the end of the first month the girls were more or less sorted into different categories. I went to work in the office as a trainer, where I was happier than in the woods, others became trainers in the woods and a very few left as they felt the life was too hard for them.

There were some scares, of course. I remember watching the trees swaying wildly one day and thinking we would have to be very careful in case one fell the wrong way. In fact, one trainer had refused to take her group out that morning in the interests of safety.

Office work began to pall so I asked if I could be released to work in the woods again. With a friend, Mary Crawford, I was then posted to Minto Estate, near Jedburgh, where we were billeted in the Laundry Cottage which was clean, warm and dry. What a blessing!

On Minto Estate, we dealt with a great variety of trees: beech (too heavy for us), Douglas fir, Scots Pine, larch and lime. The wood had to be completely cleared, with nothing left but the undergrowth by the time we had finished. There were huge bonfires of brush and branches which would burn for days and I remember one occasion when a young lad, thinking a fire was out, poured petrol on to it, only to be thrown back by the blast. There was so much heat still in it from the previous day that the fuel had ignited at once and could have badly burned the boy.

Weekends were spent mostly in Hawick, where we had friends. I vividly remember being invited to tea with two ladies whom we had met on the train from Edinburgh. A snow-white tablecloth, laid with lovely china and a wonderful meal set out for us, made a lasting impression! Another couple, evacuated from Yorkshire to Hawick, also took pity on two lonely Timber Corps girls and invited us to visit them each weekend. We were the only WTC girls in the area and therefore quite isolated.

There were many glorious days, even in winter, when the scenery was quite beautiful: spider's webs, glistening in the frost, trees, stark and coated with rime, their branches a picture with the winter sun silhouetting them against a blue sky. The Cheviots seemed to bear the brunt of the weather as often an approaching storm would come to nothing.

For many days in the winter months my friend and I would be left to our own devices, mostly peeling felled trees which had already been snedded. This was easy in the spring and summer but we hated it in winter, when it was like breaking through cement. At least it kept us warm!

Alison McLure

On Minto Estate we had horses working in the woods which were a great asset. We loved their gleaming coats and admired the way the men looked after their harness, polishing it till it shone. They cared for these animals so well.

One incident which really upset me occurred when I was given a huge tree to sned. It had been raining heavily the previous night so the bark was slippery and my axe skidded, struck a knot and swung round and hit my nose. I was rushed to Hassendean Station where the doctor stitched it for me so competently that there is not a mark today.

A transfer to a sawmill on Tyningham Estate in East Lothian was my next and last posting. I did not enjoy the work there nearly as much as the varied tasks on Minto Estate.

I still keep in touch with friends from those far off days and enjoy a journey down memory lane.

AGNES MORRISON
(NÉE SMALL)

I awoke one night to find a hedgehog sharing my pillow!

In 1940, I received my calling up papers and, along with a friend, went to the Recruiting Office in Bank Street, Inverness. The lady at the desk informed us that if we had not made up our minds about applying for any particular service the Ministry of Supply urgently required timber measurers. I think the word 'urgently' fired us with enthusiasm and the hand of fate led us to that office in Church Street where we were joined by another four girls, equally inspired, and that was the beginning of four years moving around the north and west of Scotland measuring and counting trees on various estates.

We commenced work under the late Andrew Crawford, Acquisitions Officer for the North Division of the Ministry of Supply Home Grown Timber Department, who had been loaned from his factorship of Glengarry Estate for the duration of the war. Mr Crawford was an extremely dedicated forester and took the task of controlling four young, female, novice timber measurers very seriously, making us work very hard indeed. He was, however, a kindly person and reasonably considerate of our limitations. He was in charge of us for a year and then was succeeded by Affleck Gray as Acquisitions Officer. The scene changed quite remarkably when he took over. To begin with, we were inclined to be a bit wary of the new broom as he seemed to be in a higher sphere, and had us a bit bamboozled with his Forestry knowledge. However, that phase quickly passed and we discovered that he was really a very

1. Shandford Lodge training centre, 1942. Photo from the effects of the late Marjory Stark, via Bonny Macadam.

2. Instructors at Shandford Lodge, 1943. Back row: Marjory Stark, Morag Mackenzie, Bonny Macadam, Jean Macnaughton. Middle: Betty Croll, Jessie Cameron (Camp Commandant), Eildon McConnell (Welfare Officer), Bob Allison, Isa McColl. Front: Molly Sinclair, Anne Kiddie, ?, Nan McLean. Photo: Bonny Macadam.

3. Shandford Lodge: trainees ready for work. Kittie MacAllister centre. Photo: Bonny Macadam.

4. Trainees at Shandford with Bob Allison.
Photo: Bonny Macadam.

5 and 6. Sisters Bella and Mamie Williamson pose in their new WTC uniform, Grantown-on-Spey, 1942.

7. Bonny Macadam on her first weekend home, showing off new uniform.

8. Marjory Stark. Photo via Bonny Macadam.

9. Laying-in with the axe at Bowmont, 1944/45. Photo from the effects of Marjory Stark, via Bonny Macadam

10. Jean Mcnaughton and the late Cathie Brow cross-cutting at Kinclaven in 1943. Photo: Jean Buntin (Macnaughton).

11. Snedding. Photo: Bonny Macadam

12. Dangerous work at the sawbench.
Photo: Bonny Macadam.

13. Loading at Bowmont. Marjory Stark standing on lorry.
Photo from the effects of Marjory Stark, via Bonny
Macadam.

14. Inverarnan, Loch Lomond. Working with horses Prince and Nipper. Marion Vickers on right. Photo: Marion Vickers.

15. Inverarnan, Loch Lomond, 1943. Marion Vickers with Prince, tying chains on to a felled tree. Photo: Marion Vickers.

16. Pit props at Auchterblair, Carrbridge.
Photo: Bella Nolan.

17. Another scene at the sawbench.
Photo: Bonny Macadam.

18. Rafting in Loch Voil. From *Meet the Members*.

19. Group at Glendoick Camp, Perthshire, 1943.
Photo: Bonny Macadam.

20. Glen Camp, Innerleithen. Margaret Law second from
left in back row, with cook's arm through hers.
Photo: Margaret Law.

21. WTC parade in Inverness, 1943. Photo: Bella Nolan.

22. Parade in Blairgowrie, 1943, with interesting vehicle -
bringing in Christmas trees? Photo: Bonny Macadam.

23. Another wartime group. Front row: ?, Betty Croll, Nan MacLean, Kitty MacAllister, ?. Photo: Bonny Macadam.

24. A visit to Kinnoull Hill, Perth to look at current methods employed by the Forestry Commission was included in the 1990 Reunion Day. Sue Williams (right) demonstrates a power saw. Photo: *Courier and Advertiser.*

forthright type with a ready sense of humour which was often a great asset to us, especially on wet days when conditions in the woods were anything but pleasant and we needed a bit of jollying along. His anecdotes and remarks were so highly amusing that our naturally good spirits quickly recovered.

We spent about two years under Affleck Gray's supervision, and on the whole they were carefree and happy days but, having said that, we took no liberties with our boss and he liked to see the work being done carefully and efficiently. In retrospect, he liked to think that he was unfailingly considerate! We certainly blessed him on a few occasions when, after a particularly hard morning, we were allowed to bask in the sun for a few hours with the loch water lapping our aching feet and relaxing tired limbs.

My thoughts go back to Achnacarry Estate, in the west of Scotland, where we had to assess the volume of several miles of mature Scots Pine in Glen Mallie and some timber along the shores of Loch Arkaig. When we worked in Glen Mallie, getting to the job, after a time, meant a long slog up and down the glen every day to reach the starting point. The floor of the forest had an undergrowth of tall bracken covering hazardous boulders, and the steep slope was riven with deep gullies. Added to this, we were constantly in trepidation of encountering adders, but it was not all bad and we had a good deal of amusement.

When the daily journey up and down the glen became too arduous and time-wasting we moved lock, stock and barrel by horse and cart along the rough track to a disused cottage near the head of the glen, and here we lived, or should I stay survived, for two weeks. I awoke one night to find a hedgehog sharing my pillow. I suppose I could have had worse!

Along the shores of Loch Arkaig the timber was in fragmented groups, rather than an unbroken stretch of forest, and transport was now by a boat, borrowed from the Estate, dubiously seaworthy and fitted with a temperamental outboard motor. As often as not we had to use the oars. Swarms of clegs (horse flies) and midgies did their best to devour us and I can think of nothing more debilitating than trying to row a boat and swat ravenous insects at the same time!

We did not receive any uniform at the time of registering for war service and had to use our own civilian clothes. We did get uniforms eventually – coat, blouse, green pullover, khaki breeches and green beret. Unfortunately, I have no badges, but I think they were in the shape of a spruce tree.

Apparently, members working in England were fêted by American GIs and lavished with silk stockings, chocolates and possibly some rations to eke out their own meagre supplies. The only entertainment I can recall at Achnacarry is of two ENSA concerts in Achnacarry Hall, laid on for the Commandos who were in training there at the time.

Elsewhere, if we were anywhere near a village we attended an occasional dance, concert or whist drive. Apart from that, we had little recreation.

Looking back to those years, I think we all had the satisfaction of achieving so much for the war effort. The drudgery of winter hardships was fully compensated for by the joys and freedom of the open air in Spring and Summer.

I still have my certificate from Her Majesty the Queen thanking me for my services to my country.

Footnote by Affleck Gray:

At Achnacarry I was required to report our daily position of work to Colonel Vaughan, the Commanding Officer of the training Commandos. He was a notable character, much liked and much respected by all who were under his command, and about whom a splendid biography was written after the war ended. His reply was always a cheerful, 'That'll be all right, old boy. We shan't be anywhere near you'. Nevertheless, we were occasionally alarmed by live bullets thudding into trees quite near us, and then the thump and roar of mortars so near that we had to lie flat on the ground and cover our ears.

I recall once at lunchtime sitting on a log, munching a hunk of bread and cheese, when, suddenly, an American Commando seemed noiselessly to rise up out of the ground at my feet and stealthily crawl on. As he passed me, he looked in anguish at my bread and cheese and murmured, 'Oh bo-o-oy. I could eat a *horse* right now.'

Agnes has reminded me of quite an amusing contretemps at Garve Hotel in Ross-shire when we were assessing a wood on Garve Estate. The girls, whose subsistence allowance when they were working away from home was derisive, could afford, only occasionally, the luxury of hotel accommodation and had to make do with lodgings or boarding houses in any village we might be near. My subsistence allowance was rather better and I could afford to use hotels occasionally. Out in the wilds, I just mucked in with them in whatever insalubrious bothy or vacant cottage that would shelter us.

The late Miss M., who was proprietress at Garve Hotel at the time, was well known as something of a termagant and, when I called with the team to book them in, she was aghast at the very idea of such a motley gang as guests. 'How could I', she asked, 'seat rough girls like that in my dining room with such as Admiral Dalton who is retired, but comes here every year for the fishing?'

'Miss M.' I said very stiffly, 'I must inform you that all of those whom you describe as rough-looking girls are wearing their working uniforms with honour, are all cultured University graduates doing a job of vital importance for the war effort, and one of them is in fact the daughter of a serving Admiral.' This was not strictly true, of course, but I thought that the means justified the end. Agnes Morrison and Chris Turner were hair stylists; the others with jobs I cannot recall. The 'Admiral's Daughter' was uppercrust with an Honours degree from Oxford University, but I don't think she was an Admiral's daughter! She adapted and mixed well with the others and she was strong, willing and a good worker. She was, of course, under the same discipline as the others and sought no favours. Miss M. climbed down after hearing all this and said that she could provide attic accommodation. I demurred and said that I'd had a quick look at her Register and it appeared that she was not fully booked.

'I want reasonable bedroom accommodation, Miss M., for

my party, not rat-infested garrets (the look of horror on her face was almost laughable), and if you cannot agree to granting a reasonable request I shall not ask for the use of your telephone. I shall, however, go along to the telephone box and phone my Head Office. I don't think that the Ministry of Supply will be too happy to learn of such an obstruction to the war effort and there is, of course, always the possibility of a press leak.' That deflated the lady immediately and the girls were shown to nice comfortable bedrooms. As for myself, I was so angry that I would not book in, but went up the road a quarter of a mile and stayed with Mrs MacLean, a very dear old lady whom I had known for quite a time. It did not, however, deter me from calling in at night to see that all was well and having a dram.

In the event, the old Admiral was delighted with the company of such charming young ladies and made himself most agreeable. If he had happened to question the Oxford lady about her antecedents, I am quite sure that she would have had all the resources to parry his questions.

J MOAR

She realised why the lorry had stopped!

Firstly, I must put the record straight. I'm a male! However, I did rub shoulders with some of the Timber Corps girls in the Blacklock and Kincraig areas who were billeted at Muckrach Lodge in Dulnain Bridge. Most of the girls seemed to come from the Glasgow area. Although I'd heard of girls wielding axes and saws, I never actually witnessed this. Most of the girls I encountered cleared and burned brushwood and measured timber. There were two exceptions in my experience: Margaret McQuire who drove a lorry at Nethy Bridge and Morag Breingan who extracted timber with a D6 caterpillar tractor at Kinveachy. I think I would be right in saying that the felling of really heavy timber was exclusively the province of men.

Weekly dances in the Craiglynn Hotel in Grantown-on-Spey and the odd hop in local villages helped with their social life. Willie Anderson, forester at Nethy Bridge, played the saxophone in the band at Grantown-on-Spey. Romances, of course, flourished. Ann McLaughlin became Mrs McGillivray when she married a farmer from near Boat-of-Garten and Ethel Christie became Mrs Wall when she married Micky, an Irish lorry-driver at Blacklock. I remember, too, a fellow McIver who was the Divisional Officer with his HQ in Grantown-on-Spey. I have no recollections of a Benevolent Society being in operation, but I do remember the Forestry Commission starting a Benevolent Fund in the late fifties which was discontinued in the early seventies. Ninepence a week was levied and ten shillings a week augmented one's wages during illness.

Burning Brush

The chaps from Blacklock frequently shared the same transport as the girls from Muckrach Lodge when returning from Grantown where we'd spent an evening on different pursuits. The picture house, of course, was a big attraction and quite a number found their way there. If the last bus had gone, we had to depend on the Newfoundlanders' lorry to give us a lift back. This, they were always willing to do and, after dropping off the girls at the Lodge, they dropped off the Blacklock contingent two and a half miles further up the road towards Carrbridge.

One such journey I can recount, which caused some amusement but also a bit of embarrassment to one of the girls, was the occasion when we did a journey back from Cromdale one Sunday night. The village is four miles from Grantown-on-Spey and the army was billeted in Balmenach Distillery there. The soldiers made an effort to mix with the local community and encouraged visits when off duty. The entertainment was not entirely free as we paid the going price for the drink bill. Local publicans must have frowned at this unlicensed trade!

Some of the male visitors had over-indulged and a stop had to be made on the return journey. As if by some pre-arranged deal the lorry pulled up. No one spoke as several of the men descended from the lorry, although the men who managed to contain themselves understood the situation. One girl, more curious than the others, left her seat and ventured to the back of the lorry and looked round the side. She recoiled with a startled gasp and retreated to the interior, having realised why the lorry had stopped! She must have been glad of the darkness to hide her blushes!

Our dismissal notices from the HGTPD said that owing to the contraction of the Department's operations, our services would no longer be required. We then learned that tidying-up work would be carried out by German PoWs for the next few months. Imagine our feelings! Although I wrote an irate letter to the *Sunday Post* and received five bob for my effort, it gained me nothing!

Timber!

TIMBER
IS ESSENTIAL

Help us
by returning
empties
promptly

One of Britain's Best Beers

GREENHEAD BREWERY · GLASGOW
CROFT-AN-RIGH BREWERY · EDINBURGH

CONSTANCE CAMPBELL

Coming home with dungarees, sticky with resin.

My sister Mabel Fraser, who sadly died in 1986, served with
the Women's Timber Corps. I can remember so well her
coming home with dungarees sticky with resin and very
difficult to clean. She was billeted at Muckrach Lodge near
Dulnain Bridge. Before his call-up in 1945 my husband,
Andrew Campbell, was a driver with the Forestry Commission, taking away the wood which the WTC had cut.

Nan MacLean

I have never forgotten the sight of Loch Venachar that morning.

When my call-up papers arrived in 1942, I went to register in Bothwell Street in Glasgow. A post in the ATS was offered to me but I preferred to work in the open air, after spending eleven years in an office. The Land Army was the next suggestion but, as I did not really want to work with animals, that was out. The newly formed Women's Timber Corps was the next option and it appealed to me.

Six weeks' training in Glen Etive followed this decision, which my parents were not at all sure about. I loved Glen Etive, and what a change it was for city girls to go out in the evenings to watch the deer! There was no uniform till we had finished our training and I ruined my good Burberry in that time. The 'bum-freezer', as we called the greatcoat, was not an adequate replacement! I think we must have kept the Elastoplast company in business in those first weeks, as none of us had ever swung an axe before and using a heavy six-pounder was not easy on the hands. A mansion house at the head of Glen Etive was our training base, to which we travelled on the back of a lorry, twelve miles up a rocky road.

The isolation in that magical glen did not bother us, as we were so tired at nights we just sat and chatted, while knitting, before falling into our narrow beds. I vowed then that I would never sleep again in a single bed!

My first post, after training, was to Balquhidder on Loch Voil, near Strathyre, where I worked in the office at first, making up the wages and calculating the income tax. You would have thought that it was going into my pocket the way some people complained! We were driven on a tractor down to Strathyre forest where the WTC girls felled the smaller trees: Douglas fir, pine and larch. We also peeled the tall trees for telegraph poles. On Loch Voil, the logs were sometimes 'rafted' out but I was never involved in rafting. There was more social life there: dances in Callander and whist drives, run by the Red Cross, in Sir James Wilson's house.

After four months at Strathyre, I went to Invertrossachs, on Loch Venachar, where I remained for the rest of the war, as camp supervisor. One of the 'perks' was sleeping beside the stove in the Nissen hut, which became very cold in the winter! There was no coal, but we used to go down the road to an RASC camp, when it was unoccupied, and keep the guards talking while others filled up the bogie with their ration of coal!

Sometimes, we would hear bangs during the night and know that someone was poaching salmon. Next day the police would come and ask if we had been offered any. Some hope! The poachers sold the salmon to the hotels.

At Invertrossachs, I worked both in the woods and in the office, where I was responsible for ordering the camp provisions with our caterer's licence. Some girls, who did not take sugar in tea, would ask if they could have the sugar to take home and were none too pleased when I pointed out the large spoonful that had gone on to the porridge! Breakfast was always porridge and dried scrambled egg. Some cooks were good with dried egg and some made it seem like a piece of leather! There was always plenty of bread, butter and marmalade and, for dinner at night, plenty of potatoes with the boiling beef from the soup, filled us up. The girls were so hungry they would sit down to eat without even washing their hands! In fact, in winter we were reluctant to wash at all! Sometimes, in winter mornings, we would use the water from our hot water bottles which, at least, had the chill off it! In the autumn, the falling leaves would choke the water tank and there would be no water at all. We had to take all these problems in our stride.

On one occasion, the cook at the men's camp did not turn up and we were asked for volunteers to help out with their breakfast. Nobody wanted to get up at 5 am so I went myself. I have never forgotten the sight of Loch Venachar that morning. It was quite awe-inspiring in its calm beauty, with the sun rising over the surrounding hills.

At that camp, we had adopted a dog, with one eye blue and the other brown, aptly naming him 'Timber!'. He was of the '57 varieties' type and could do everything but talk. From the estate of a gentleman who died, I remember acquiring a tall mirror, a baby grand piano, a gramophone and some easy chairs for the camp, making it look more homely. 'Timber!' used to admire himself in the mirror along with a kitten we had.

A tree once fell on my arm and I was taken to Stirling Royal Infirmary. I still have trouble with my shoulder and perhaps should have filled in a compensation form as I had done for others.

At Invertrossachs, I was responsible for the moral and physical welfare of the girls so I arranged for them to have visitors in the camp rather than going out and feeling romantic, with a full moon shining on the loch! There was no trouble that way. Some girls were quite young but I stood no nonsense! The men's camp was two miles away which was far enough for safety!

There was a German PoW camp at Comrie and they used to come to transport timber from us. One day, in my ignorance, I said to a German, slowly and clearly, in a loud voice 'You . . . sign . . . here.' He replied in fluent English 'Yes, thank you very much', making me feel very small! We had all wanted to do something for the war effort but, only sometimes, did it dawn on us that the lads we replaced were away fighting, while we enjoyed the freedom of the woods. It was not sensible to dwell on it.

Money was very short and I remember once, at a dance in Callander, winning an elimination waltz and a prize of £1, with which I started a savings account. Out of their wages the girls had to pay for accommodation and food. I was responsible for the catering so I always tried to keep the food bill as low as possible in order to give them as much spending money

Issue of

new

RATION BOOKS

YOU NEED 1. Your present Ration Book with Reference leaf filled in.

2. Your Identity Card.

WHERE TO GO

MIDDLE CHURCH HALL, TAY STREET, PERTH.

as possible. Some girls even managed to save a little and send money home.

All the girls in the camps in the west came from the west coast and the Glasgow area. Many had been shop assistants in the big Glasgow stores: Pettigrew and Stephen, Copland and Lye and Dalys. There was no 'March Past' arranged for us as in the east coast in Edinburgh, Dundee and Perth, but I did attend a reunion of WLA and WTC in the Kelvin Hall in 1974. The majority of girls were hard-working but only through example; if you stopped, they stopped. I used to think if one walked into the loch the others would follow!

In 1946, everyone went back to their old lives. I went back to Bremners for a while, before getting a travelling job. However, I did miss the camaraderie of the WTC, though I still have so many memories of that unusual life, into which so many girls were thrown.

Margaret Law

We helped with the peats in return for a home baked supper!

I volunteered for service in the WTC after reading posters asking for people to join the war effort. After a month of training at Brechin, I was posted to the Glen camp at Innerleithen to help to fell trees, then on to Gorebridge to a sawmill and from there to Shinness, Lairg, tree-felling again. In Gorebridge, I was in private digs but in the other two places it was hutted accommodation. The huts were heated with wood-burning stoves which gave out a good heat when lit but the place soon cooled down at night. We used to take it in turns in the winter to stoke the stoves all night – strictly against the rules, of course! The ablutions were pretty primitive in some camps. When you wanted a shower you had to ask a friend to turn on the cold tap which was conveniently situated outside the shower! No luxuries such as hot showers for the WTC!

The social life was not very exciting but we did have good laughs sitting round the fire. Occasionally, we arranged dances and invited the local folk along. At the Glen camp, we sometimes had the company of Canadians, Australians and New Zealanders who came on leave and stayed at the Glen House. In Lairg, we helped with the peats in return for a 'home-baked' supper!

The work was very exhausting but, as I enjoyed being outdoors and the company was good, I adapted fairly quickly. The important thing was the feeling of friendship.

I was demobbed in December 1945 and have never regretted my days in the Timber Corps.

MARGARET QUARTERMAN
(NÉE STEPHEN)

The camp was in a clearing in a large forest.

As my age group was one of the first for compulsory call-up to women for war work, I received my call-up papers, aged twenty, in March 1941. I decided that instead of "armed forces" I was going to join the Women's Land Army. Before the date on which I had been asked to present myself, I saw in large print in the local Evening News a request for women volunteers to work in a department of the Forestry Commission called the Women's Forestry Service. I thought it sounded interesting so I called at Drumsheugh Gardens, Edinburgh, in my lunch hour.

After leaving school, I worked as a cashier in Boots the Chemist on Princes Street. A few minutes walk from there were the Forestry Commission offices, where I was interviewed by a lady who explained what I would be expected to do. I said I would like to volunteer so she took my name and address and said she would be in touch.

So, in July 1941, I was on my way to Blairgowrie, in Perthshire, by train, with several other girls bound for the same destination. We were met by a member of the Forestry Commission who took us to the camp at Meiklour, a few miles from Blairgowrie. The camp was in a clearing of a large forest and consisted of four wooden huts: two living and sleeping quarters, a dining-kitchen hut and an ablutions hut. All were very sparsely furnished. The sleeping quarters had beds and blankets and were heated by wood-burning stoves.

On the first morning, we were taken into the forest where a lot of felled trees were lying. We were given a narrow spade, sharpened on both sides, and shown how to strip the bark from the trees by the most efficient method. I remember it was a hot summer and, with blisters on our hands, aching backs from bending and sunburn on our exposed skin, we were not too happy! After a few days a number of the girls returned home, but I stuck it out and, as more men were needed for active service, the peeling of the bark was stopped and we were gradually introduced to the felling of timber. We went through the whole procedure of laying-in, felling and sawing into required lengths, mostly for pit props and telegraph poles for army communication.

After a few months at Meiklour, I went to a camp at Kinnordy near Kirriemuir. In the autumn of 1942, it was decided to start a training school for women of the newly formed Women's Timber Corps and I was asked if I would accept a position as an instructor there. A large house, Shandford Lodge, had been taken over at a place called Fern, near Brechin in Angus. The village of Fern consisted of a few houses, a shop and post office, a small school, a church and two farms, one of which was Shandford.

This was so successful as a training centre that another camp was set up at Park House, Drumoak, to which I was posted in March 1943. In February 1944, when it was decided to end recruitment, the training camps were closed and, as I was getting married in June 1944, I went to a private contractor in Peebles for my last few weeks in the WTC.

On looking back, it was an experience I would not have missed for the world. Many of the friendships we made were for life.

MARY WEIR
(NÉE LOCHEAD)

The rope broke and the bogie went hurtling down off the rails!

I started work in August 1942 for a private timber firm in Kilfinan, Argyll.

My first job was digging ditches and rebuilding dykes. After that I worked at the sawmill as tailsman to the sawmiller, clearing slabs, measuring and transporting timber to Arrocher Station over the old 'Rest and be Thankful'. Negotiating the hair-pin bend was always a worry. I was working on the cross-cut saw with my boss one day when he cut off a finger. It was a horrible sight. I was at Kilfinan for about fifteen months. The farmer and his wife at Drum Farm were very good to me, providing tea twice a day.

I then went to Pitlochry with the same firm, where we were just felling, no sawmill. I stayed with a Mr and Mrs Grant. He was the gamekeeper in Baledmund. We were cutting at Balnakeilly. One day a sad thing happened. The woodcutters were felling in Baledmund policies and, unknown to them, the Laird's two grand-nieces, on holiday from Findhorn, were playing nearby when a tree was felled and one of them was killed. It was a sad time. Perhaps they had not heard the cry of **'Timber!'**.

Mr Andrew Ferguson, who owned the estate was a very generous man. He gave us knives with 'Baledmund 1944' engraved on them.

On a happier note, my first landlady gave a party for my twenty-first birthday. That was at 'Kirk Lodge', where Mr Alex Pirnie, our horseman, lived. One day, two of the men were at the station with a load and, when they came back, they said they had been speaking to Allan Weir from Kilfinan area. I said I didn't know him, but finally I met him in 1946 and married him! He was working in Ballinluig at that time.

When the work was finished in Pitlochry, I moved to Glenstriven camp, in Argyll, where I stayed in Inverchaolain Lodge which was quite comfortable, with cheerful log fires. Annie was cook and Jean was supervisor.

The wood was shipped out by puffer. I remember one day we were loading and the bogies were being let down by a winch on a wire rope from the tractor. Jenny Amos (Laird) was on the tractor, I was at the top measuring and Betty, Jimmy and Callum were on the pier. Suddenly, the rope broke and the bogie went hurtling down off the rails. Betty and Jimmy jumped into the boat but Callum was knocked off the pier into the water. We were all scared and ran to the shore to see Callum coming out of the water with his cap still on. We had a laugh about that, but he was shocked and wasn't able to work for a while.

I remember when the war finished we all got into the lorry and went to Hopper's Pier and danced. It was wonderful.

I want to finish with the story of our cap badge. In recent years I worked in the antique trade. One day a lawyer, who collects cap badges, came in to see if we had any. I said, 'No, but Mr Brown have you got this one?' He was very interested because he had never seen a WTC badge. He wanted to buy it

but I refused his offer. I have had it for over fifty years and didn't want to part with it. He said that if ever I did he would give me a good price. Later on, two dealers came in looking for cap badges. I showed them my badge and they were very anxious to have it. They went from £25 to £45 to £75 and I said 'No' but one of them said 'Tell her why we want it.' 'Well, I had one,' I was told, 'and sold it to an English dealer who put it to auction in London and got £375 for it because they are so rare.' I said I had been to my reunion recently and lots of ladies still had their badges. He replied, 'That's why they are so scarce!'

JEAN 'STEVIE' ROBERTSON
(NÉE STEVENSON)

The ladies of Brechin deserve a mention.

Having just read a book by an English ex-member of the WTC about life in the Corps in England and Wales, we seem to have been more fortunate in Scotland in being a better organised team of woodchoppers who worked very hard and I am sure that lots of us are still going strong. My partner, when we first joined the WTC, was also Jean so, to save confusion, this was changed, in my case to 'Stevie' and hers to 'Swannie'. My funniest memory of Swannie is of her coming down to breakfast one morning and asking someone to scratch her back. A mouse shot out and cleared the room before any one of us had time to scream!

My experiences in the WTC lasted from 1942 until disbandment in 1946. I was posted first of all to the Forestry Commission, after suffering the Luftwaffe raids on Clydebank and deciding it would take more than German bombs to remove me! A batch of nine girls was transported to Bamff Estate at Alyth in Angus, but four of them decided that rural life was not their scene and threw in the towel at an early stage.

Bamff estate consisted of four huts, each containing ten 'jills' from Dundee, Perth, Glasgow and Edinburgh. There were outside ablutions and a dining hut with a cook and supervisor to care for us. Eventually we moved into Bamff House with the kind permission of Mr Ramsay.

After a spell of cross-cutting and snedding, I worked at the saw-mill before being promoted to dragging logs with 'Spider', a huge Belgian horse.

Timber!

My next stop was Roughmount, an all-female camp, where there was a railway line through the forest on which a hot meal was brought to us each day – while the German prisoners-of-war looked on, with only a half loaf of bread and a small cube of cheese for sustenance. We really had no complaints about the food: plenty of cheese and spam; the NAAFI was always open and the fish and chip shop in Forfar provided variety. The ladies of Brechin deserve a mention as they were very kind to us; providing a real 'home from home' when needed.

Then on to Glenmoriston where we worked in the nursery, weeding and lining out the young plants which were then distributed to various forests for planting. In winter, we did 'brashing' to keep the roadside bracken-free, in case of fire. Along with two others, I stayed on with the Forestry Commission after disbandment and finally finished at Glenmoriston with Jim McEwan, the Head Forester. I met my husband there and married into the Forestry Commission for the next forty-five years! We moved to Skye, then retired to Maryburgh in Ross-shire, an area where my husband had been a Chief Forester before transferring to Skye.

I have never regretted my decision to 'go for trees'. Despite all the drudgery and hard work, I enjoyed the experience and made lasting friendships. I still correspond with Rose Simpson (Tich), in Dundee, and Rose Miller, in Glasgow. Rose

CHEESE

Starting on April 2nd, the cheese ration is 2 oz. a week instead of 3 oz. This makes it more than ever important to see that each member of the household gets his or her own share. It doesn't matter whether you use it plain or cooked, as long as it's " equal shares " for everyone.

ISSUED BY THE MINISTRY OF FOOD

Miller's sister was in another division of the WTC. Another friend, Alice MacGregor, lives in Inverness now but came from Perth originally. There were no medals but how can that be compared to all the fresh air in the sweet smelling woods?

We all attended the 1990, '91 and '92 reunions of the WTC in Perth, when it was quite an experience guessing who was who and reminiscing about those far-off days.

MARY BOUNAUITO
(NÉE DALY)

She always listened to us when we were homesick.

I spent three years in the Women's Timber Corps at Shandford Lodge during the years of the war and I would like to pay a warm tribute to Babs Dewar, our leader, both in the hut and in the forest where she took great care of us. She gave us plenty of good advice, always listened to us when we were homesick and made the hut feel like home.

Even after the war, in her home town of Burntisland, where she married Trum Hutton, she took care of people. I always kept in touch with her, even after moving to America, but, sadly, she died the year before I returned to Scotland, after the death of my husband. Babs Dewar had a heart of gold and I know every girl who was at Shandford would want to join me in paying this brief tribute to the memory of a selfless, caring leader.

MARGARET FRASER
(NÉE BREINGAN)

They registered our entrance by playing 'The Woodchoppers' Ball'.

When war broke out in 1939, I was only fourteen years old and still in school in Clydebank. I was relatively unaffected by the war until 1941 when my mother died, following a stroke, at the early age of thirty-nine. She was buried the day before the first blitz on the Clyde.

My father was a foreman with Rolls Royce and, after leaving school, I went to work in the Singer Sewing Machine Company in the wages department, where I eventually became a comptometer operator.

As a lover of the outdoors, I enlisted in the Timber Corps in 1943 and was sent to Shandford Lodge for training. After the basic training, I specialised in driving tractors and caterpillars. When I was considered to be competent, I was transferred to Park House on Deeside to extract timber from Park House Estate.

My next posting was to the Altnamain area, lying on the Struie road which runs from Alness to Bonar Bridge. With my office experience, I was assigned to clerical duties on this camp. Although the camp lay in a remote part of the Highlands, the close proximity of a Canadian Forestry Corps unit enabled us to have an exciting social life, as they offered us transport to dances in Alness and the surrounding villages. The renowned Canadian Corps Orchestra, who played at the dances, invariably registered our entrance by playing 'The Woodchoppers' Ball'. Love was in the air for most of the girls, and I was no exception! We girls were greatly outnumbered and much sought after. On one memorable occasion, I arranged to meet with two gentlemen admirers at the same time but, luckily, one of my girl friends came to the rescue and made up a foursome.

Life was not just a social whirl, of course, and we laboured hard, extracting timber for pit props and railway sleepers. At weekends we were expected to take turns at cooking the meals. For the most part, this did not pose a problem, but two of our members, from the Western Isles, could not participate fully for religious reasons, leaving some weekends somewhat disorganised.

While I was there, I was befriended by the Ross family who welcomed me into their home. Mr Ross was a sawmiller on base. He was an exceptional man who, although he had lost an arm in an accident, was still able to do the work of two men. I remain most appreciative of their hospitality.

My next posting was not very enjoyable. I was transferred to the Grantown Division, but based at Advie and, therefore, isolated from the group. It was a lonely assignment. By this time, I was driving a D6 Caterpillar, and was once called out to rescue an army vehicle which had run off the road between Grantown and Forres, near Huntly's Cave. While I was at Advie I was in contact with prisoners-of-war for the first time. They were Italians and not very easy to get on with.

After a thankfully brief stay in Advie, I was transferred to the Cromdale area, residing in the Dunvegan Hotel in Grantown.

From 1940 till 1945 the army occupied Muckrach Lodge, near Dulnain Bridge, which had, in pre-war years, been an exclusive, private shooting lodge. The gardener, William Fraser, was to become my father-in-law. When the army vacated the premises the Women's Timber Corps moved in, giving about twenty-five girls the privilege of living in relative luxury. I continued to drive various heavy machines, DZ, TD9, and D6 Caterpillars, working the area around Nethybridge, Kinveachy and Alvie. In addition to the luxury of living in the Lodge, as a 'Cat' driver, exposed to diesel fuel, I was allowed the privilege of a daily bath!

As a result of an accident at work in 1946, I met my future

MINISTRY **MF** OF FOOD

SOAP
RATIONING

FROM MONDAY, FEBRUARY 9TH, soap may be bought only against a coupon or buying permit. The oils and fats used in soap manufacture occupy much shipping space, and some of this must be saved for food. You will have 4 coupons in each 4-weekly period, and will be able to use these how and when you like within the period. There will be no registration, and you may buy from any shop stocking the kind you require.

Each of the four coupons which make up a four-weeks' ration will entitle you to any one of the following :—

either
4 ozs. Hard Soap (common Household Soap in bars or pieces)
or 3 ozs. Toilet Soap
or 3 ozs. Soap Flakes or Chips
or 6 ozs. Soap Powder No. 1
or 12 ozs. Soap Powder No. 2
or 6 ozs. Soft Soap.

husband. While I was hauling wood with a D6, the timber suddenly struck a stump, snapping the drag chain which whipped back and struck me on the face below my right eye. The injury required sutures and a brief sick leave. I busied myself at the Lodge with chores and, while cutting sticks one day, the gardener's son, Sandy, home on leave from the Royal Marines, offered to help me. Romance blossomed and we kept in touch for the remainder of the war.

In late 1946, I was demobbed and returned home to Clydebank where I was re-employed by the Singer Company for a time. Sandy and I were married in Glasgow and returned to the Spey Valley to establish our home and bring up our family in Nethybridge, surrounded by the hills and forests where I spent my happy years in the Women's Timber Corps. 1997 marked our fiftieth wedding anniversary and fifty-one years since leaving the WTC.

Time moves on but memories remain.

JEAN STEWART

We taught the local girls Ballroom dances.

During the spring of 1943, I was billeted in Ardbrecknish Manse overlooking Loch Awe, having joined the Women's Timber Corps to do my war service.

Most of the girls came from the Glasgow area and our main job was stacking pit props. There was a men's camp two miles up the road from the manse. Their job was tree-felling, cutting the trees into lengths and then, using horses, dragging the felled trees out of the wood. Mr Dow was in charge of the unit and decided that there was no reason why the WTC should not play a greater part in the work in the woods – work that was traditionally for men only. Eventually, he had a squad of girls who could turn their hand to all but the heaviest of tasks. Shouts of 'Timber!' would ring out along the lochside and we would hear the crash of another tree hitting the ground. Rafting was also done on Loch Awe where the hillsides were very steep and it was difficult to get lorries in to pick up the timber. WTC girls were involved in this too, creating rafts of logs to be towed away by boat to loading points for collection.

The town girls were quite an education for the locals and they, in turn, taught us about country life. All the dances held locally were Scottish country dances which we quickly mastered while, in turn, we taught the local girls Ballroom dances: Quickstep, Slow Fox-trot and Tango. We went to dances in Port Sonachan and Cladich and even crossed by boat to Kilchrennan. It could be quite dangerous on windy days as the loch is very narrow at that point.

Although we were often cold and wet, and eaten by

"Timber!"

midgies, I can look back on these days with a smile. Our only claim to fame was a parade of all the services through Glasgow to the City Chambers where we were inspected by a civil dignitary and invited into the Chambers for tea. I think this was in 1944.

MARIE HENDERSON
(NEE DICK)

. . . the scent of spruce and pine all around.

Walking along Shandwick Place in Edinburgh one afternoon in June 1942, I saw photographs of girls working in the woods in a shop window and thought 'That's for me!' They looked so happy and, as I was on the point of making up my mind about war service, it seemed to solve my problem.

On the first day of July, I left the Caledonian Station, changed at Ladybank in Fife, changed again at Perth, changed again at Coupar Angus, then arriving at last in Blairgowrie, I got a bus to the camp at Meiklour. What a memorable journey!

When I first joined the Women's Timber Corps I was asked to bring my own working clothes and footwear. However, I was later supplied with a uniform similar to that of the Land Army: boots, dungarees, breeches, shirts, pullover, a great-coat and a green beret. The camp at Meiklour in Perthshire had few luxuries; not even flush toilets or proper wash-hand basins at first! At night, after a hard day's work, we often had to chop wood for the wood-burning stove and hope to have some hot water in two hours. I remember the pipe which ran from the stove to the roof becoming red-hot as we tried to heat the hut on cold, winter nights. We used to heat old flat irons on top of the stove and rub them up and down the sheets to warm our beds. There were no electric blankets then!

On my first morning, I was assigned to a squad and handed a four and a half pound axe and told to watch the others! After a few weeks, I could lay-in, sned and cross-cut as if I had been doing it all my life! I really enjoyed this new life.

Marie Henderson

In January 1943, some of us were sent to Ethie camp, just outside Arbroath. I was there for a short time only, as a friend at Glendoick camp persuaded me to apply for a transfer and join her there. It was a very happy camp and some of us have remained friends ever since.

At Meiklour and Ethie only the men worked at stacking and on the saw bench, but at Glendoick each squad got a turn at the saw bench and at stacking the logs, ready for the lorry to come and transport them to the station. I once worked at the station, loading wagons which had previously been used for coal. You can imagine how we looked at the end of the day!

'Pieces' for our midday break were made up at breakfast time and we made tea in a dixie on a wood fire. Once, we tried syrup tins but it was difficult to pour the tea from them. Sometimes, we were given pies which we would heat on a shovel over the fire. They tasted horribly of smoke but the fresh air and hard work made us so hungry that we ate them anyway! The newspapers were full of exhortations not to waste food. 'Waste the food and help the Hun', said one poster.

On a Saturday, if there was no social activity, we stayed in camp to sharpen the axes and once we had a lesson on sharpening cross-cut saws.

In the winter of 1944, there was a particularly bad snow storm at Roughmount which blocked the roads, preventing food vans from reaching ever-hungry girls. Some of us decided to try to walk the three miles to Tannadice station only to find, on arrival, that there were no trains running. However, we got to Dundee on the snow-plough engine and from there caught a bus to Perth, where there was hardly any snow, and at last purchased some food. After that, we were all sent home until the snow disappeared. On our return to Roughmount we found snow still lying in the woods and the huts were cold and damp. But we were young and soon got back into our routine.

We had two parades in 1943. The first was in Edinburgh for the Timber Corps only. Afterwards, we had tea at the City

Timber!

Chambers, a big treat! The other was for all the Services in Perth on June 5th, 1943. A Sergeant Major from the Black Watch came to drill us for the parades. Some of the girls just could not get the hang of it at first, but on the day of the parade we were complimented on our performance.

Glendoick camp closed in September 1944 and eight of us were posted to Meiklour, so I was back where I had started. We were all sorry to leave Glendoick. Four of us had met our future husbands there!

A memory of those days which will remain with me always is walking into the woods to work, early in the morning, with the scent of the pine and spruce trees all around.

MARIE C F DICK

TO A FRIEND

The whispering of tall pines,
Swaying in a pale blue sky,
The rippling gleaming lochan -
These things will never die.

A well-loved path across the hill,
A sheep-track through the heather,
The river rushing down the glen -
These things go on for ever.

The pale new moon shining o'er the moor,
All this since the world's beginnings;
We are born, we live, we die -
But life is sweeter because of these things.

Nan Brown
(NEÉ SMITH)

Tea was made in a dixie over a fire.

When my call-up papers arrived in 1942 I was working in a shop in Edinburgh. Whatever I chose was going to be a big change in my life so, eventually, I decided upon the newly formed Women's Timber Corps.

Forty of us arrived at Shandford Lodge, near Brechin, for training. At first, I found the work very hard but, encouraged by the similar plight of the others, I soon got used to the outdoor life. We were taught to 'lay-in' a tree, fell it with a cross-cut saw then sned it. The lorries came to be loaded, so we helped with that too. After a month's training, we were posted to different forestry camps all over Scotland. My first camp was Dunphail, near Forres, which seemed a long way away from my home in Edinburgh.

The work at Dunphail was varied: loading tractor bogies and driving the wood to the station where it was loaded on to railway wagons, felling and snedding; and burning the brushwood. The whole day was spent in the woods, taking our lunch break where we worked. Tea was made in a dixie over the fire and sandwiches were eaten sitting on a log. Each camp had a cook so there was an evening meal ready for us after work.

On summer evenings, we went for walks and on Saturdays sometimes went to a local dance in Forres or Elgin.

After five months at Dunphail I was sent to Glendoick, near Perth. There, we were allowed to use the saw-bench at which we sawed the logs into pit props, measured them, then stacked them in piles according to size. I was sent to work as 'tailsman' at the sawmill, where I met my future husband.

Later in 1944 I was sent to Meiklour, a few miles from Blairgowrie, and then, finally, I was transferred to Roughmount camp, near Tannadice in Angus. I was there for only a few months before leaving the WTC at the end of March 1945 prior to my marriage to John Brown, whom I had met at Glendoick.

I have many happy memories of the Timber Corps and still keep in touch with friends made all those years ago.

You never know who's listening!

CARELESS TALK COSTS LIVES

JESSIE MACKAY

I played a farewell tune on the bagpipes – 'Leaving Glenurquhart'

In 1942 I joined the WTC and worked at Inchbea, near Garve, for about two years. The work was very hard there, but we also had many happy times. The girls were all from the Island of Lewis except one, Isobel Kennedy from Loch Luichart, who later became Mrs Sprunt.

My memory is not very clear, but I think it was in early 1943 that four of us were transferred to Corriemony in Glenurquhart where we remained for only a short time. I seem to remember that we finished off by cutting right above the falls with the Hydro-Electric power station far below with a hundred foot ladder going down to it. We were quite sad leaving there and I remember the lorry waiting while I was persuaded to play a farewell tune on the bagpipes! The tune was the march 'Leaving Glenurquhart'.

We were then on our way to join our friends from Inchbea at Craigdarroch Lodge, Contin, to start cutting the wood at Rogie Falls. The first job there was cutting down trees to form a loading bank. At one stage we were felling Douglas Firs at Strathgarve and what big awkward trees they were!

My friends stayed on in Craigdarroch after Rogie and worked in Kinellan Wood at Strathpeffer but I became unwell and had to be discharged. I took up work as a ward orderly in the County Hospital which was then in the old Spa Hotel in Strathpeffer, now demolished. I would indeed have attended the reunion in Perth, but not knowing if any of my former colleagues would be there, I decided not to go. Later, I got a phone call from one of them, Mary MacDonald, now Mrs Mary Mackay from Lochs, Lewis, who regretted that we didn't go together. We joked that we never got any medals. I must contact her again if there is another reunion. We may be able to attend together.

My experiences, apart from the usual pranks and risks we took, were very few but, looking back, I would not have changed anything. The girls were a grand bunch and true friends. We shared our joys and sorrows and helped one another through difficult times.

FIREWOOD—CROSS-CUT SLABS FOR SALE

(EX CANADIAN FORESTRY SAWMILLS AT KILTARLITY AND DOCHFOUR)

The Ministry of Supply, Home Grown Timber Production Department, Edinburgh, have arranged with MACDONALD & MORRISON (INVER-NESS), LIMITED, and others, for the Distribution of the Firewood on the following basis—54/- Cash for a 3 Ton Capacity Motor Lorry Load (heaped up), Delivered in Bulk at Buyer's Address in or around Inverness.

Buyers must, however, arrange for their own Storage at their own Expense. It is also clearly understood same is not to be Sold by Weight (No Hardwood Firewood Blocks are available).

Orders should be given earliest possible, to give Distributors a chance to arrange Delivery in a reasonable time. For further particulars, apply at—

MACDONALD & MORRISON (Inverness) LTD.

23 CHURCH STREET, INVERNESS

Telegrams—"MORRISON"   Phone 1388 (3 lines)

MOLLY PATERSON

Others ran behind me till I mastered the bicycle!

A Ministry of Supply unit was operating at Ardbrecknish, near Dalmally, Argyll under the direction of Mr Stewart Dow and a contingent of WTC was billeted in the Ardbrecknish Manse. I had been working in Dundee, contracted mumps and was sent home to Cladich to recuperate and as soon as I was able, joined the WTC two miles away.

My duties were mainly clerical; timber measurer, wages clerk and all general office work. I greatly enjoyed the companionship of a lovely, lively bunch of girls, mostly from the Glasgow area. I can still remember most of their names and often wonder where they all are. I still correspond with a friend who lives in Bridge of Weir.

I spent as much time as I could at the Manse, where we had a lot of fun, despite the war. One girl tried to teach me ballroom dancing to the one gramophone record she possessed till we were shouted down by the others. Others ran for miles behind me till I was able to master a bicycle! We walked miles to the dances in Port Sonachan, and even crossed Loch Awe in a rowing boat, in the pitch dark, to dances in Kilchrenan. We still had to be at work early next morning. How vividly I remember the blisters on my heels caused by the thick woollen socks and heavy 'tacketty' leather shoes as I walked one and a half miles to work each day.

I have so many memories, all happy, of life in the Women's Timber Corps.

MARION VICKERS
(NEÉ McINTOSH)

Hi Honey! Making for the Sahara?

When I received my call-up papers in 1941 I reported to the Labour Exchange at Alexandria. I was instructed to report to Charlie Miller, who was the Operations Foreman between Luss and Arden on Loch Lomond side. This was a women's camp where six local girls were employed, dragging timber with horses and peeling logs.

Along with another girl, I was given a horse for hauling the smaller trees. I also drove a caterpillar. After some basic instruction, I was soon accustomed to dealing with horses. The first horse I had was a vicious old draft horse, used for hauling beer barrels in Dundee, who had feet like soup plates and a great hollow in his back. One evening I was riding back to camp when I met a group of Americans who hailed me, 'Hi Honey! Making for the Sahara?' I can still feel the embarrass-ment! However, I soon had my eye on another horse called 'Nipper'. Mr Miller said I would never handle 'Nipper', but I had other ideas!

With Italian prisoners-of-war, I was on the lorry driving timber to Kildarven Station. We then moved to Daligan Wood, then on to Rubha Mor when I had to cycle four miles to work every morning. The next move was to a timber operation at Inverarnan, at the head of Loch Lomond. The horses were stabled at Arnburn and I had to walk 'Nipper' the twenty-nine miles on the public road to the head of Loch Lomond, where another stable had been erected.

There was no camp at this site and the men were trans-ported to the job by lorry. When I started work in the wood I

123

Another Load Ready

was quite lightweight and not in a robust state of health but, although the work was hard, I loved it and seemed to thrive on it. Often, arriving home from work, my mother had to scrape the mud off me with a knife. Eventually I became stronger, to the extent that the men referred to me as two-ton-Tessie! However, I didn't mind a moment of it and how I loved my horse.

Three years later, when my husband and I were travelling up the A9 near Calvine, I suddenly shouted, 'Stop, isn't that Nipper in the field?' And sure enough, when I called 'Nippy, Nippy' he came at a trot and knew me at once. I wanted to return regularly with tit-bits for him but, sadly, the farmer who was grazing him said he was soon to go to the slaughter house.

The atmosphere in our camp was always good. I remember our rather correct District Officer entering the wood at a side entrance and surprising some of the men eating their 'piece' before lunch-time. He complained to Charlie Miller who, having a heart of gold, replied, 'It's just like this Mr W., we eat when we are hungry and we drink when we are dry.' We thought this was very bold of Charlie, but it gave us a good laugh!

In our camp we had to supply our own working clothes and for some reason I never received a WTC uniform. When the WTC was disbanded, we received no gratuities to re-furbish our wardrobes and scant thanks for our considerable contribution to the war effort. While this remains a sore point with all the members of the Women's Timber Corps I know, I would not have missed the experience for the world. To this day I have retained my love of trees and plants and my garden remains a source of joy to me.

Extra Coupons

FOR MANY

MANUAL WORKERS

Many types of workers can now claim a special issue of 10 extra clothing coupons.

The trades and occupations elligible for this supplement are set out in leaflet G.O.S. 10. This is now obtainable - by employers, self-employed workers and trade union officials ONLY - from local offices of the Ministry of Labour and National Service, and employers are asked to post copies on works' notice boards. The list of eligible workers will also be displayed on posters at Employment Exchanges and elsewhere.

ISSUED BY THE BOARD OF TRADE

MAMIE GILLIES
(NEÉ MCKILLOP)

It was a lovely wee camp, despite no 'mod cons'.

I was one of the Shandford Babes and never have I forgotten my very happy days as a 'lumberjill'.

After my training, I was posted to Dumfriesshire where a new camp was being opened at Wallaceton but, as it wasn't ready, I stayed at another camp called Newtonairds where I met the six girls who were going to Wallaceton. We worked for the Forestry Commission before the Ministry of Supply took over so, with my friend, Morag, from Shandford and the six girls, we arrived at Wallaceton and stayed in private digs until the building was completed. The eight of us stayed at the camp from opening until it closed and, in later years, most of us have met again.

The camp had four huts for accommodation, with a hut for kitchen and dining room. We had all 'mod cons', with wood stoves in our hut and plenty of firewood, running hot and cold water and shower units in the ablution hut.

We travelled by lorry to the woods. The biggest wood was Crawfordton where we hiked up the hill to fell timber. The bottom of the hill had the saw bench and the stack yard.

The Glencairn was a beautiful spot where we walked across the valley to Maxwelton Braes and the big House, Maxwelton House, where Annie Laurie had lived.

We cut down many other plantations around Moniaive and made many friends in the process. Some of us had bicycles, which made it easier to get around. Saturday was our big day when we got a bus to Dumfries, so our social life was good.

Timber!

Maxwelton House was used by the Norwegian Army and Navy boys recovering from war wounds, and some worked in the woods. Latterly, we had German PoWs working in the woods, but not with us.

When Wallaceton closed we were posted to other camps. With two friends, I went to the Speyside Inverdruie Camp, Rothiemurchus, near Aviemore. The timber was very heavy and mostly the men felled. My friend, Ethel, and I were fortunate to get some felling, thinning out a wood. There was a saw-mill where some girls worked, that burned down while we lived at Inverdruie.

It was a lovely wee camp, despite no 'mod cons'; old tilly lamps, the toilet was a corrugated shed with a hole in the ground, and there was no running hot water or shower units in the ablution hut. In spite of this, I loved the camp and could look out of the window, when lying in bed, to the Cairngorm mountains. When it closed, I moved on to Muckrach Lodge, Dulnain Bridge near Grantown-on-Spey.

I missed the huts as everyone was close together there, but in this lodge we all had small bedrooms. My days as a lumberjill came to an end at Muckrach Lodge when the war was over.

I went back to Lanarkshire to a village called High Blantyre where I joined the Scottish Youth Hostels and spent most weekends wandering the countryside. I also started Scottish country dancing which I still do as a member of the Royal Scottish Country Dance Society.

When I married, I came to Glendaruel to a lovely glen where I was still surrounded by trees. So I have spent half a lifetime here and never felt lonely. My husband died six years ago, but I have a son and daughter who live close to me.

MARGARET GRANT
(NEÉ TAYLOR)

We loved Glen Etive . . .

Before the war, I was studying music, as I wanted to be a singer. My teacher was a man called Ian Waite, who had studied with Dame Clara Butt. Hearing me singing in a corridor one day, Ian decided that I ought to sing professionally and, as I could not afford to study without working, I obtained employment in the printing department of Glasgow Corporation in John Street. This was working very nicely until they sent around the forms asking which service you wanted to join. For years, before the war started, I had been attending meetings of the 'peace pledge' union. I was an idealistic little pacifist and wrote to say I was not joining any service! Then I began to think that they would send me to something I would hate, so I thought I would join Forestry, which seemed to be in keeping with my pacifist views. I discovered, however, that it was the Home Grown Timber Production Department that I had been assigned to cutting down trees, not planting them!

I was pushing a pen one Wednesday night, before being taken on a bus and dropped at the bottom of the Buachaille on Rannoch Moor on a January day in 1942. With a foot of snow on the ground, I was just dumped there and by the Friday I was shovelling gravel in a river bed with a big navvy's shovel! You are sore, you are tired, you are hungry and you are unable to think, you just feel things. I shut off completely. That was in January. Then, one April morning in Glen Etive was so beautiful, with snow on the mountain tops and a turquoise blue sky with pink fluffy clouds, that I suddenly realised I was a big healthy lump, about ten stone of muscle, and that life was wonderful. I had had to contend with all of this when I was not thinking at all, but that morning I started to think again and I loved it. And I loved Glen Etive which was, at that time, a very isolated glen. We lived in a big old mansion house which has since been demolished.

Glen Etive was principally a training camp where Geordie Maxwell was the boss. 'You do the shoving and I'll do the grunting,' he would say! When we had finished six weeks of learning the arts of forestry we were sent out from there to other camps.

At one point, Geordie decided that we should only do a job for a certain time because I saw a girl getting her fingers off. I was tailing on the big saw in the mill and throwing down the short ends to her which she was putting through a liner, blethering all the while, and then she said 'Look what I've done,' and held up her fingers which were spouting blood. Geordie decided that we should do a job only for a couple of weeks because our concentration was lapsing if we spent too long on the same job.

I worked a horse on drag roads; I felled and burned hag. When a tree is felled you have to brash it, get all the branches off, before it is cut and stacked. The branches are often left over the winter, piled up in heaps and then burned. You get showered with ticks when you set fire to them. We used to have 'tick-picking' sessions, picking the ticks off each other! When they're small they are reasonably easy to remove; nasty little things, sucking your blood.

We were all very reluctant to go, because we loved Glen Etive, which is a most dramatic glen: Deirdre's glen, 'Deirdre of the Sorrows'. A lot of the timber was taken down. There was a funny wee tug boat that puffed up Loch Awe, with a wee man called Captain Burns, who had a twinkle in his eye for all the young lassies! A lot of the timber went down by boat to Taynault to the station. Some of it went out through the glen to Dalmally, but I was never on that lorry.

I've some very sad memories of Glen Etive too. The lad I was engaged to, from Sussex, suddenly appeared in this isolated glen to see me. He walked all the way and then I had to wave to him from the top of a mountain, as he was going down to catch Captain Burns' boat. That was the last I saw of him, for he was killed in 1943.

I was posted to Loch Aweside, to Ardbrecknish, to the old manse, which looks a bit like a council house stuck on a hillside. I grew to love Ardbrecknish in spite of my reluctance to go there. I had been a climber all my life and there were so many mountains there to prowl over. There, I met a lovely country man, Archie Stewart. I thought my grandmother had taught me everything about birds, bees, fishes and flowers when I was young, but Archie taught me more about nature. He was a man who could spot a bird miles away. He knew the names of animals, birds and wild flowers and knew where rare plants grew, which interested me greatly.

There were six of us there at first but more came later. Apparently, the women who had been working in Ardbrecknish had got a very bad name for having soldiers in their beds and they were being replaced by six 'good' girls from Glen Etive! I think there were about ten girls in that house.

I didn't want to love Loch Aweside. Ben Cruachan separated me from Glen Etive and the bedroom that I was given, upstairs in the manse, looked right across to the Ben but I grew to love this view as I worked with Archie. If volunteers were required for anything awful, like cutting blows, that is where there had been a terrible storm and, in a wood, the trees had fallen and were hanging over each other, Archie and I would go. It is a fairly dangerous job because you have to work with blocks and winches, cut bits, listen for creaks and then push in wedges. You need a tractor for winching out. One of the jobs Archie and I did together was cutting this gully of blows. He would be sitting on his tractor, winching when I gave a signal but, because it was in a gully, sometimes the load would get its nose into a bank, meaning that I had to get down there, arms up to the top in mud and loosen the chains and push him up a bit so that he could lift the head. Archie would be sitting there, puffing on his pipe and I could not reach for my cigarettes at all, so I got more and more bad tempered. Then, one Friday night, Archie said to me, 'You're a bad tempered bitch and I'm going to sort you out on Monday morning.' I didn't know what he was talking about! He arrived on Monday with a clay pipe and a twist of tobacco and said, 'Try that!' I thought he had gone mad but I smoked that pipe for two years and never thought anything of it, until the first time I went home on leave and took out the pipe on the train and, watching the faces, wondered why they were all looking at me so strangely! Then, when I got home my grandmother said, 'You're getting coarse, girl'. I had probably developed very bad, unladylike habits, through wearing breeches and, perhaps, was sitting with my leg over the arm of a chair!

Rafting was done in two particular places. One, Inishail, a little island in the middle of Loch Awe, that we called 'The Green Island', though in Gaelic it means the stately, charming isle, was heavily wooded with tall larches and spruce. The bracken up from the shore grew shoulder high and in the centre were the ruins of an old monastery. At one end, sheltered by trees and overgrown with roses and briar, was a tiny burial place with old, old stones, like the ones in Iona. We worked on this island, cutting wood, so there should have been a great deal of noise. I used to stop and listen for the ring of axes and muffled crashes, the clanging of chains and the clumping of horses on the brown and peaty drag road, the crackling and hissing of fires burning and the hammering of iron 'dogs' into the rafts; sounds of beasts and humans working together though it never sounded like another work-a-day wood. The sound seemed to be enveloped and taken up as if there were a great blanket of silence over everything. The quietness was a wonderful experience. We used to talk jokingly about the peace but everyone felt it, even the men, though some of them would have laughed at the idea if you suggested that they were sensitive to atmosphere. Another unusual thing we all noticed was that the animals loved that island; they thrived there. These were solid, hard working, timber horses which usually grazed quietly but there, they used to play and did not even use the stable we built for them. The horses were swum over at the start and we went over by boat to work each day. We did rafting from the 'Green Island' across to the Lochawe village side, the opposite side from which we were living.

We also rafted from Port Sonachan, a beautiful place where there is a hill on which we had cut all the timber, right across to Kilchrenan on the other side. I loved rafting: standing in the water in waders with a big hammer through your belt, the chain from the raft over your shoulder, with 'dogs', rings with spikes on them, and the men coming down with the horses. With the rings they would drag the 'swing tree' in to the water, loosen the load and push the timber towards you so you could catch it, take another dog onto the chain, bang it into the log and thread it on to the raft. Each log is attached by a bit of chain running through the ring of these dogs. One of these times, I nearly drowned because a fellow had just unloosened his load and floated it towards me and his horse had started off to go up the track again. He didn't notice that the hook on the swing tree had caught onto the chain, just under the water, which was over my shoulder and, as the horse walked away, this whole thing tightened and the load came towards me. When you are under water, with timber above your head, you suddenly lose your sense of place, which way is up and which way is out. However, the next man coming down hauled me out. I could have drowned quite easily, if he had not been coming down. I can swim, but I was struggling away under there losing my sense of direction. I was worried about the chain, but there was no terrible sense of panic. Maybe, drowning is not as bad as you think. The next thing I was aware of, was being battered on the back by a couple of the men and lying, sodden beside a fire on the shore.

Bovay, the wood of the cow, was an incredible wood. I saw an astonishing thing there. The wood was in such a mess and the river bed, in the summer we were working there, seemed very low. We often used the stones to walk up, because of the mess of timber, until one day when we were threading our way up the river and Jock MacVain suddenly said 'Get away from the river, get away!' He was shouting his head off and we didn't know what he was on about. However, when Jock spoke urgently we all reacted quickly, scrambling out of that river bed just before the most thunderous sound and this wall of stones, twigs and water came rushing down. If we had stayed there, we would all have been killed. Apparently, a storm had created a dam away up at the top and it suddenly broke. It was an awesome sight.

We went one Christmas Day to work near a farm house and because the snow was fairly deep where we were cutting and clearing, we decided to go and ask Mrs Mac, who lived opposite the pass of Brander, if we could use her loo. She said it was just down at the bottom of the garden and there was this lovely little hut, with a heart shape cut out of the door and inside a polished plank with two holes cut out of it and the river down below! In fact, I was so interested that, years later, I did one of my lectures on the story of the loo.

Swing trees and chains lay outside, which was a fine arrangement, till a frosty morning when you picked up the chain without thinking and it stuck to your hand and away would come the flesh. Agony! But there were all sorts of lovely things. Woods in springtime are idyllic places with the young larches a special shade of yellow-green. And summer evenings when we finished for the day and stood on the pier waiting for the boat from Taycreggan to Port Sonachan, shouting over our order for the hotel to have our shandies ready, are occasions never to be forgotten.

The last thing I thought I would be was an interior designer. The room I was billeted in, in the old manse on Loch Aweside, was Victorian in decor; it had a blue room, a green room and I was in the red room. I used to waken up every morning feeling like Christian with his burden, so one day, I said to Mr Dow, the boss, 'If I can find some paint somewhere, can I change this?' All I could get was yellow and green. However, the girls I roomed with started dying sheets to make lavender curtains and bed covers. Everybody admired it so much that we started decorating the whole house. When we finished, it was sunshine yellow with bits of green here and there. The ceiling was in a mess and somebody had stuck bits of putty in so I pasted stars over the putty. Years later, when my husband and I tried to buy it, these marks were still visible. That was the first of interior decoration but the first of interior design was when a farmer came one day and said his wife walked miles in the kitchen, a big farmhouse kitchen, and he asked if I would organise the kitchen for them. I had always done drawing and water colour painting when I was up there but that was the first bit of design I had tried. We fitted in the decorating in the evenings as we were all fighting fit. I don't remember anyone being ill.

Our cook was a lovely little woman from Islay, called Flora, who married one of the head fellers, Bertie Cooper. Flora could make things out of nothing so the food was absolutely wonderful. When I started doing this interior design thing for the villagers, I was paid in butter and eggs and the odd rabbit, which Archie would supply, or even a hen sometimes. So we ate well! We made up our own sandwiches for lunch but Flora would make up all sorts of exciting things, like a kind of sandwich spread, made of vegetables, which she would make up herself. We made our own tea in the woods. Sometimes we took out onions because the smell of onions frying outside is just wonderful!

We had Saturday afternoons and Sundays off. A lot of us sang. We had one lovely girl with grey hair. Mary had been sent to us, as quite a number of people were, from Clydebank. After a raid, she was the only one left alive in an Anderson shelter. Her family, the animals, big dogs were killed all around her and the doctors decided, when Mary recovered, that working in a job like ours would be good for her. She had a wonderful singing voice. We used to sing in the local hotel. One day I was down in the hotel using the telephone, as there was no phone in the house, and I was singing in a long corridor, which was like singing in your bath, 'Softly Wakes my Heart' from Samson and Delilah and, at the other end of the corridor, a man appeared and joined in and I remember saying to him, 'You like music too.' I was speaking to the Director of Music for Lanarkshire, Neil Lees! Neil became a particular friend of the girls and would teach us to sing. He played at concerts and on a Sunday some of us would go down and sing at the concerts. It was great fun! We used to sing in the local memorial church, St James, just down the road from the manse and were allowed to play the organ and sing when there was no-one there. In fact, it had twin bells and these were the bells that we rang when we discovered the war was over. Herbert Ruddy was an old Irishman, whom we would find sitting under a tree at breaktimes reading 'Sturm' reflections, German philosophy, the last thing under the sun that you would expect an old woodsman to be reading. He and I pulled these bells until the wires broke! One morning, we were sitting at Cladich, waiting for the lorry to arrive, when Mrs Stewart, the postmistress came out and said 'By the way, the war is finished', and we all went mad! We collected timber to light bonfires on the hills up and down Loch Aweside and rang bells in every wee church. The owners of Sonachan estate had kept fireworks from before the war, so we had a wonderful fireworks display.

In January of 1946, I decided to go to the Glasgow School of Art to study Interior Design. There, I stayed for the rest of my career, first as a Lecturer in Interior Design and eventually as Head of the Department.

Sturm und Drang – storm and stress. This was a literary movement originating in Germany in the late eighteenth century.

LENA PAYNE
(NÉE LAURIE)

We were always known as Blackie and Ginger.

My experience began with training at Park House, Drumoak, in Aberdeenshire. Along with another girl, I was posted to Stonehaven where we were billeted in a family home. We, therefore, never experienced camp life and remained there from 1943 until disbandment.

Every morning a lorry picked us up and took us to our place of work. We started in Ury estate, went from there to Cormant and then to Netherley where there was a saw-mill which employed some of the older local men and boys. There were also four women whose husbands were in the forces.

Over the years, I worked in the saw-mill stacking planks and in the woods cutting pit props. Occasionally, we part-nered the lorry drivers to the railway station with the timber. For most of the period my friend, Helen Miller, and I were partners, felling trees, snedding and cross-cutting them.

During that time we were on piece-work and, after all the clearances, there was always the burning of the brushwood. We were reasonably fit because during our training we spent half the day on fitness training and the other half in the wood, although we still received a bit of ragging from the males. I remember the Bon Accord newspaper having an article about the WTC and publishing pictures of us at work and doing our keep-fit exercises. That led to some teasing!

We didn't work with men until our posting and Helen and I were always known as 'Blackie' and 'Ginger' because of our hair colour.

Our social life was similar to that of the local girls; going to the pictures, dancing and to Stonehaven Swimming Club. It was a different experience to girls living in a camp.

At the start of the training we were kitted out with overalls and boots and on completion of the course we were given a coat, a green beret, two pullovers, one pair of boots, one pair of shoes and a shirt.

I actually joined the WTC rather than being called up because my dread was being directed compulsorily to a munitions factory far from home (see poster below).

MAVIS F DANKS
(NÉE WILLIAMS)

I might just lobby the Queen!

Not wanting to 'pen-push' in another service I initially applied to join the Land Army, although I didn't like cows! After an extensive interview, I was told that there was a move to establish a Timber Corps for which a slightly higher academic qualification was required and, as I was thought to be a suitable candidate, I didn't ever join the Land Army. This new Corps was being inaugurated by the Ministry of Supply in order to release able-bodied men from the forests and sawmills for active service.

Being in the first one hundred and twenty recruits, I received a WLA uniform, including the hat. The WLA was under the Ministry of Agriculture, Fisheries and Food (MAFF) but the Timber Corps came under the Ministry of Supply. When I became a forewoman, I was paid as a civil servant.

No coupons were taken for uniform and the minimum kit was issued: shoes, greatcoat, puttees, pullover, breeches, socks, shirts and a hat with a badge bearing a wheat sheaf. Later, trainees were issued with green berets with a fir tree badge when they enrolled. When my uniform arrived it was far too large as I am only four feet eleven and a half inches. You can picture the breeches on me! Luckily, my father was a master tailor and altered them to fit me. My nickname in the WTC was 'Tich'!

Some of the original land girls worked in the woods without training and were later drafted into the Timber Corps. They worked untrained until 1942 when

Timber!

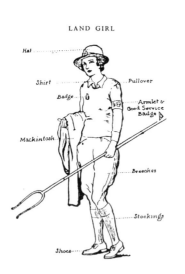

LAND GIRL

Hat
Shirt
Badge
Pullover
Armlet &
Good Service
Badge
Mackintosh
Breeches
Stockings
Shoes

THE UNIFORM

Overall-coat
Dungarees
Gum boots

the WTC was formed. The memory of the camaraderie in those war years has lived with me always. There was fun, friendship, hardship and kindness; all making a lasting impression.

Footnote
In 1994 Mavis Danks published her own account of her experiences in the Women's Timber Corps, south of the border. The book is called *Lumber Jill*.

MURIEL WATT
(NÉE WHYTE)

The factor enjoyed our seven-layer steamed pudding!

As newly graduated students of Aberdeen University, twenty of us volunteered to work for the Forestry Commission for one month. We were given accommodation at a shooting lodge on Sir Arthur Grant's Estate at Monymusk, near Aberdeen.

Eighteen of the group used to collect branches in the forest while two cooked breakfast and dinner for the ravenous girls and made them substantial packed lunches. Everyone was exhausted by the end of the day.

We enjoyed the work and it was a happy break before our real war work began. The factor came once for dinner and enjoyed our seven-layer steamed suet syrup pudding, as well as the young company! These were memorable days, although not directly connected to the Women's Timber Corps.

JESSIE MACLEAN
(NÉE ANDERSON)

We were a' Jock Tamson's bairns!

My camp was at Wallaceton, Dumfriesshire, a memorable area of Burns and the Maxwelton Braes of Annie Laurie, which are indeed bonnie. I was in complete ignorance of real war and the horrors being enacted in France and Germany, so it was a very happy period of my life, surrounded by the beauty, peace and a sort of romantic atmosphere, as each passing day presented a different scene, in stark contrast to the action in Europe. Most girls at Wallaceton were either from Glasgow or Edinburgh and shared great camaraderie at camp and in the woods of Crawfordton, Dalmacallan, Dunreggan and Craigdarroch. We did all we were trained to do: felling, snedding, horse, tractor and saw-bench work, stacking, peeling, loading the lorry, which was driven to the wee station at Glencairn. I hated the stackyard, and even now I only remember the bitter cold, wet days and the mud – not the glorious variety! Felling was my favourite activity and I look with scorn at to-day's lumber-jacks with their noisy power saws.

We all worked well together and camp life was grand for girls from different backgrounds with different dreams and ambitions. We were a' Jock Tamson's bairns! At Wallaceton we even experienced a really romantic event. A dashing soldier from overseas appeared one morning to claim his bride. Banns were immediately called from the steps of the local church and at mid-day the happy couple were married. What excitement! In 1943, I went to training school, Park House, Drumoak, Aberdeenshire, where an entirely new way of life opened up for me; tentatively making new friends from all over, and eventually forming our own wee cliques and finding out about each other's backgrounds, ambitions and hopes. Everything was so new for all of us; having huts as our home and sharing with about twenty girls. Daunting as this experience undoubtedly was, we soon got used to each other and came to respect and enjoy each other's company immensely. I remember the names of leader girls, such as the well known Margery Stark, affectionately known as 'Starkie', Betty MacDonald and Effie Gray. Our 'Chief Executive' was Mrs Burton. At Wallaceton, our boss was the late Jock Mitchell, a quiet and extremely nice, approachable man. Mait McGhee was the foreman, a rough and tough, big chap, in appearance, but good to work with. We liked and respected them, for they knew their jobs and responsibilities. They were very decent to all of us and, for most of us, Wallaceton was everything we could have wished for, and indeed, it was truly heartbreaking to leave it in 1945. It would not have mattered where I was sent after that, I knew I would not like it! Rothiemurchus, therefore, had no appeal for me. There was nothing wrong with the camp; it just was not Wallaceton! The foreman there was the kind, fatherly figure of Mr. Munro, from Glenfeshie. Everyone was friendly and helpful but my heart was in Maxwelton Braes.

How often, when travelling about, were we asked by many members of various military units, 'What regiment are you in?' We thought this very funny indeed and went on to try to explain to them about our work: felling, snedding, peeling – oh, the pain! – saw-bench, stacking, horses and tractors. They didn't believe any of this. I remember one sailor listening in amazement to our story and his reaction, as one suddenly enlightened, 'Oh, you work for Bryant and May then, making matches!' Talk about hackles rising, for we regarded ourselves as being very special, which, of course, we certainly were!

I had gone to the local labour exchange to volunteer for the WRNS as I loved the sea and ships. Reaching this dismal office, which was 'jam-packed', I knew I'd have to wait for ages and so I had time to study the posters, plastered around all available space, depicting all manner of military service and information. One poster 'burst' into my sight. It was so lively, showing a bonnie lass wearing a green jersey, breeches, open necked shirt and amazingly, with an axe over her shoulder. I couldn't relate to this most unusual sight, something I'd never seen before and I'd never heard of the WTC. I was excited – there she was, this happy, smiling girl and in the background, mountains, trees and a loch – exceedingly romantic to me, a very naive teenager. At last, when it came to my turn to join the navy, I abandoned ship and entered the beautiful world of trees and nature.

In Wallaceton we worked for a while alongside German prisoners-of-war and, much to our surprise, they were just like ourselves! They were 'Germans', they kept on reiterating, not 'Nazis'. Indeed, there were four Nazis working in our woods under armed guard and nowhere near us, but the 'like us' Germans were decent, family men with 'snaps' to prove it; hard working and well behaved, how pitifully appreciative they were to receive a cigarette, occasionally, from the girls. As a way of thanks, they made such clever, and lovely, wooden toys for us; dogs with wagging heads and tails. My favourite was one of two girls cross-cutting a tree and this too was an action toy.

Another time there were Norwegians based in Maxwelton House who were also hard working and good company. We would organise dances at our 'rec' and they, in turn, would endeavour to reciprocate at their billet, the famous Maxwelton House. I enjoyed this liaison with the Norwegians for Norway had always intrigued me. Two of my life-long joys were associated with it, ice skating with Sonja Henie and the music of Edvard Grieg. Now I had real live Norwegians to learn from and was delighted when they taught me some of their language. In later years, I visited Grieg's house, outside Bergen, and the lovely museum, near Oslo, which Sonja Henie had left to her beloved country.

All this, and the agonies and horrors of war were still unknown to us, in our blind ignorance. All in all, it was a learning process, socially, historically and practically.

Timber!

It all seems picturesque and romantic, looking back, but it really was a 'jamboree', even then. The actual felling and snedding was competitive between pairs and the laying-in was a work of art which took long and patient practice. Even so, some of the girls never got the hang of it. We were always motivated to try harder. We considered ourselves far better than the few men working nearby, older woodsmen, who, of course, paid no attention to our 'superiority' and foolish arrogance.

Our stackyard was situated across the river Cairn from Maxwelton House, the home of Annie Laurie, and the lovely pastoral land was well known to our own famous Bard. His farm, Ellisland, was only sixteen miles from the camp. This was a place of the Covenanters also, and I loved it all. My heart is still there, but definitely not in the stackyard! Winter time in the stackyard was quite awful, ankle deep in icy mud. The logs to be cut and stacked were encrusted with this chilling, frosty muck. No amount of hand-blowing or "pine-needle" tea could alleviate the pain of frozen fingers and not even the muscle torture of peeling helped – nobody's favourite job! Yet, our lives at Wallaceton and the woods of Crawfordton, Dalmacallan, Craigdarroch and Drumdreggan remain a twenty four carat gold memory. This utterly peaceful and exciting lifestyle, broken only by the occasional shout of 'Timber!', was in total contrast to the realities of terror, agony and brutality which were taking place in Europe: blind ignorance indeed, for civilians and forces alike. We were never allowed to know. The truths are still being unfolded today.

In 1945 I left Rothiemurchus, joined the ATS and was posted to Europe. I was deeply interested in the arts, opera and architecture although, at that time, places like Stuttgart and Cologne were just fields of rubble but Venice, Capri and Vienna still shone with all their legendary magic.

When I was demobbed, my friend Mrs Simpson, who was our Chief Welfare Officer, WTC, Scotland and who corresponded with me, suggested I apply for the vacancy in the Forestry Research Assessment Party. I did, and was accepted.

Our boss was J. A. B. MacDonald. There were four of us, all ex-lumberjills, so it was an enjoyable time for me, travelling all over Scotland to woodlands and nurseries and even to a plot in Edinburgh's Botanic Gardens. I think Dr Cowan was in charge then. Our office, to which we returned for two months to catch up with the reports, was in Manor Place, Edinburgh.

Summing up, the Women's Timber Corps helped me to discover my love of travelling, as well as being responsible for a very great happiness in my life, then and now.

NEXT FRIDAY'S
W R E N   D A Y

The W.R.N.S. Interview Officer is coming to Inverness next Friday. The second Friday of every month is always "Wren Day" in Inverness. If you are thinking of applying to the Women's Royal Naval Service, call and see the Interview Officer at the N.R.O., Bank Street, from 11 a.m.—6 p.m.

BELLA NOLAN
(NÉE WILLIAMSON)

I had to hide the pan of eggs under my bed!

When I was seventeen, my first experience of working in the forest was at Drum, on the way to Glenfeshie. This was before the WTC was formed. We were involved in all kinds of work including felling and snedding although there were not many girls working there. On one occasion our foreman, Charles Stewart, expressed some doubt regarding the ability of the girls to cope with the tough work. The next day I volunteered to work a cross-cut saw with him. During the day he kept asking me if I was tired and wanted to stop but I kept going despite being quite exhausted. At the end of the day we had cut down one hundred and twenty trees! Months later a new supervisor arrived and when I volunteered for a task he said, 'It's okay, I've read about you. Your record is in the office!'

One of my most vivid memories of working at Drum is of a tragic accident when we were travelling home to Kingussie one evening. Drum was too far to walk or cycle daily so we were transported there and back. As the truck rounded a bend one of the boys, Bobby Tennant, prepared to jump off the side onto the grass verge. At the instant he jumped the truck swerved to avoid a parked car and he was trapped under the back wheels. I was first to reach him and could tell he was seriously injured. He later died in hospital.

After working at Drum, my sister, Mamie, and I had a spell at Torcroy before moving to Inshriach. Once the WTC was formed in 1942 my friend, Silvia MacKenzie, and I applied for a transfer to Auchterblair at Carrbridge. During the week we stayed at a camp at Carr Road, near enough for me to be able

148

BETTER POT-LUCK

with
Churchill
today

THAN HUMBLE PIE

under
Hitler
tomorrow

DON'T WASTE FOOD!

to return to Kingussie at weekends. The camp had three huts with at least ten beds in each one, and a separate ablutions hut which we named 'the blue lagoon'! The showers only worked occasionally. When I moved to Auchterblair, Mamie went to a camp at Muckrach Lodge, near Dulnain Bridge, where she was working with German prisoners-of-war, some of whom were as young as sixteen or seventeen.

Most of the girls at Auchterblair were from Glasgow and Edinburgh. It took them many weeks to adapt to country life but they were all very determined to succeed. We were only allowed one week's leave per year and had to work on Christmas Day. Once a week we were allowed a late pass till midnight by our supervisor, Mavis Richards, otherwise we had to be in by 10.00 p.m. with lights out at 10.30 p.m.

Despite rationing, I don't remember having too many complaints about the food, although it was very basic. Because we worked near the camp, we had three meals a day in the dining hut. Often there was soup, bread and potatoes, and occasionally there was fish.

Most of the work was making pit props and we were involved in felling, snedding, cross-cutting and dragging. It always took two girls to control a horse when the timber was being dragged out of the forest. I recall Nancy Russell and Lucy Dodsworth driving the truck which took the props to the railway station. The only jobs I didn't enjoy were sharpening blades and using the power saw because the 'kick-back' bruised your knuckles.

Because the work was so arduous we were often glad to go to bed at 10.30 p.m. but we did have a social life at weekends. If a dance was being held locally, we could stay out until 2.00 a.m. and once a week we went to the pictures in Grantown. One of the supervisor's rules was that we were not allowed out of camp wearing our wellington boots. On one occasion we were called back to change our footwear and missed the bus to Grantown, which didn't worry us because we just hitched a lift!

In the huts, we were not allowed a fire between May and October, but one week I remember bringing some eggs back from Kingussie and frying them in the hut for the girls. Mavis Richards, however, caught us and I had to hide the pan, full of cooked eggs, under my bed while 'Rich' dismantled the fire. The whole hut was full of smoke. Afterwards, we had a good feed, though.

In April 1943 we had a 'march-past' in Inverness to celebrate the first anniversary of the formation of the Timber Corps. With about one hundred girls taking part, we paraded along Bank Street in front of a crowd of spectators before being led away by the pipers and drummers of the Air Training Corps along Fraser Street, Church Street, Queensgate, Academy Street and on to the High Street. The salute was taken by Provost Hugh Mackenzie. We were then entertained to tea in the Churchill British Restaurant where we received good service badges. After each period of six months we were eligible for a good service badge.

I remember our District Officer from Auchterblair, Affleck Gray, and our Operations Foreman, Peter MacKenzie, with whom I still keep in touch.

When I left the WTC, I married a Newfoundlander, lived in Carrbridge for two years, then went to Newfoundland for two years, before returning to Scotland.

When we decided to go to Newfoundland, it was necessary to travel by sea as I was pregnant and air travel for mothers-to-be was not permitted in those days. We sailed out on the SS *Aquitania*, under Canadian command at that time, and, to our horror, found that Newfoundland husbands and wives were to be separated for the journey! I shall never forget lying in a hammock, in the hold, feeling utterly miserable. The misery was made worse when we heard that Canadian wives, travelling without their husbands, had been allocated cabins! After docking at Halifax, Nova Scotia, at midnight, we caught a train the next morning for North Sydney to get the steamer to Port aux Basques, in Newfoundland. A civic reception had been laid on for the returning Newfies in St. John's, but we were so tired we gave it a miss!

George, my husband, got a job in the American naval base in Placentia Bay. Living in the country in Newfoundland, about fifty miles from St. John's, was somewhat different from Scotland: no inside toilet, no running water. All the water had to be fetched from a well. I remember a Scottish girl saying to me that, where she was, there were only dog tracks and the only thing on wheels was the pram that she had taken from Scotland!

The people were reserved till you got to know them, but George's family were very kind to me. Newfoundland is a lovely country which, perhaps, I did not fully appreciate then. However, I have been back several times since and now love it very much.

We spent two years there and then decided to come back to this country, sailing on the maiden voyage of the SS *Nova Scotia* to Liverpool, from where we travelled north to Kingussie, to bring up our family in the Highlands.

Note: A press report of the parade in Inverness lists the girls who received good service badges. Their names may be of some interest.

Speyside Division

Matilda Anderson, Mary Anderson, May Chapman, Jean Ellis, Mabel Fraser, Jean Frew, Lindsay Frood, Margaret Fulton, Beth Gorman, Jessie Grant, May Heggie, Janet Jamieson, Jane Lobhan, Wilh. Mackay, Eliz. Macbain, May Mackenzie, Margaret Macaughtrie, Wilh. Millar, Annie Reynolds, Elexa Robb, Betty Smythe, Harriet Taylor, Margaret Walker, Rita Watt, Bella Williamson, Mary Williamson.

North Division

Janet Fairgrieve, Catherine Macdonald, Christina Macdonald, Katie Macdonald, Margaret Macdonald, Mary Macdonald, Jessie Mackay, Dolly Mackenzie, Johanna Mackenzie, Katie Mackenzie, Nora Mackenzie, Catherine Macleod, Mary Macleod (1), Mary Macleod (2), Mary Urquhart, Wilhelmina Wood.

MOLLY HOGG

If ye had a man an' weans, ye widnae hae a figur like that!

When I joined the Timber Corps my husband, Malcolm, was serving with the Royal Engineers. I thought that if I joined *when* I wanted, rather than wait to be called up, I could join *what* I wanted. So I chose the Women's Timber Corps!

Except for a day in Edinburgh or Glasgow, I had never been away from home, so Brechin, where I was asked to report, seemed very far away. I was so nervous that I ended up in sick bay on my first night at Shandford Lodge!

The first day was spent in acquiring our uniform. Work clothes consisted of huge army boots – imagine the agony after wearing high heels! – navy blue dungarees, a beige airtex shirt and a dark green jumper; for dress uniform, we wore light brown breeches, beige woollen knee-high socks, brown lacing shoes, a thick, khaki coat with brass crossed axes on the shoulders and a green tammy with a fir tree emblem on a bakelite badge bearing the inscription Timber Corps, WLA.

We were allocated to long, wooden huts each bearing the name of a castle. I was in 'Edinburgh'. Each hut had a girl in charge and it was there that I met Mary Mitchell, now Mary Ralph, who was to become a life-long friend.

The second morning brought a rude awakening! A large metal tray was banged at 5.45 a.m. and we had to jump out of bed and wash in the freezing bathroom. Washed and dressed, we then went over to the mansion-house kitchen where breakfast was served. After a good hot breakfast, sandwiches for lunch and a china tea mug were distributed along with a canvas bag in which to carry them. Then came the worst part, we were handed an axe and told to get up on to the lorry to be taken to the forest. I was so small I had to be hoisted up each time!

Training at Shandford took six weeks, during which we were taught how to fell trees using an axe and a cross-cut saw. The final test was taking down ten pine trees in a day, snedding them and burning the branches.

There was a lot of good-natured rivalry between the huts. When we took our washing in we would find faces drawn on our pants or nettles and twigs in the sleeves of our shirts. The fairies always got the blame!

The six weeks training was soon over and we were posted to different parts of the country, to sawmills and forests. I was sent to Finzean in Aberdeenshire along with three girls from other camps, two of whom were sisters from Glasgow. We shared a bedroom in a farmhouse which was a good two miles from the sawmill. Every morning and evening, rain or shine, we walked to and from work, in pitch dark in the winter months. The sisters were used to dances and cinema so they went to dances at the Canadian lumberjacks camp. Neither the other girl nor I went to these socials, preferring to stay and write letters or read. I often wonder how the sisters fared in Canada, as they got married to Canadians and went to live in the backwoods – they couldn't boil an egg at Finzean!

The girls were never allowed to use the circular saws; huge saws that ripped a tree in half and smaller ones to cut planks into different thicknesses. Our job was to stack the wood in widths by making a base of four thick planks in a square then building layers up from there going alternately in opposite directions, separated by small blocks to let the air in to dry the wood. If a mistake was made the pile would topple and it had to be taken down to the wrong plank, so we soon learnt to build correctly to satisfy the inspectors who came round to check.

One day when we were at work a terrible scream rang out and one of the men came up to me and said, 'Are they all off?' I realised what he meant when he held up his hand showing every finger slashed to the bone, having been caught in the circular saw. Someone jumped on a bike and rushed to the nearest house for towels and bandages while another summoned the boss from the hill by holding their hand on the lorry horn till he came running. I bandaged the injured hand, put on a tourniquet and put a blanket round him before he was taken to Aberdeen Infirmary. I was as cool as a cucumber! Everyone said how well I had done! Then I rushed round to the back of the shed and was very sick! The fingers were saved.

The men at Finzean had never had women working with them before so, when nature called, they just went into the woods, but now something had to be done for the girls. They decided to build a wee hut over a burn by first laying two tree trunks across the burn and building the hut on top of them. One of the men then said to an unsuspecting girl, named Clarisse, 'Sit on this plank for a moment.' He took a pencil and drew round her bottom and cut out the shape. We did have a good laugh!

I always sang as I was working, one of my favourites being 'You are my Sunshine'. To this day I get letters from a dear friend, Bella, starting 'Dear Sunshine'.

After Finzean closed down, I was sent to a sawmill at Doune which was great as I could get a train there from my home in Dunblane. My last move was to Keir, near Dunblane, where we felled trees, burned brushwood and sometimes went to Dunblane station with loads of timber which were loaded on to long flat trucks. Not long after that, the war ended and we all went back to our own homes. My greatest fear at Finzean was that the war would finish when we were up on the moors and nobody would remember to tell us!

In 1974 I attended a reunion of the WTC and the WLA in the Kelvin Hall in Glasgow to which former members came from all the corners of the world.

During the meeting a lady strutted on to the stage to show that she could still get into her uniform. For a moment there was silence as we wondered if we would have dared, then a broad Glasgow voice shouted, 'Are ye mairret?' The reply was, 'No, I am not.' 'That accoonts fur it then. If ye had a man an' weans ye widnae hae a figur like that and ye widnae get intae the uniform!' Everyone cheered!

It was wonderful to meet people after so many years. I have so many happy memories of the Women's Timber Corps.

Cook or radio-locator
comfort makes your chances greater!
Wolsey undies, streamlined, slick,
keep you cool and trim and quick!

~ ~ ~ ~ ~

When on leave be truly chic!
Wolsey frocks make strong men weak!

Wolsey Ltd. Leicester

Wolsey

MORAG SHORTHOUSE
(NÉE MACKENZIE)

If you go down to the woods today. . .

You would not have found any teddy bears in 1942 but, possibly, a group of girls sitting on a log, beside a brushwood fire, waiting for a large dixie to come to the boil. A ration of tea would then be added with care and the girls would come and fill their mugs, add their own sugar and drink the tea whilst eating their cheese or spam sandwiches. After half an hour, they would go back to work felling trees, cross-cutting, snedding, burning brush, working the sawmill or loading a lorry. Yes, this was the Women's Timber Corps.

At the end of 1941, I knew I would soon be eligible for war service so I went along to the Labour Exchange in Stirling to explore the possibilities. I got papers to fill in for the WRNS but, on the way out, saw a poster of a girl in breeches asking for volunteers to work in the woods in the Women's Forestry Service, the forerunner of the WTC. As I had always been interested in plants and trees, I went back and asked about the work. I was given a form to fill in and after an interview was told to report to Meiklour, near Blairgowrie, in February 1942. A friend, Jean Stewart, joined up with me and, being given the same travelling date, we left Stirling station together carrying suitcases full of warm clothes in which to do our training. On arrival we were shown our hut, allocated a bed and a wooden locker like a broom cupboard and told to report to the dining hut when we had unpacked to meet the other girls. They arrived back from work and, after we had introduced ourselves, there was a mad rush to wash before supper. I never saw food disappear so fast in my life!

Timber!

Next morning, we set off for the woods where Mr Allison, the head instructor, explained what had to be done and issued us with saws and, to start with, two and a half pound axes. Eventually, I used a five or even a six pound axe. We were shown how to 'lay in' a tree; making a mouth in it the way it was required to fall. Then we got a cross-cut saw and sawed the tree down; satisfying work with a sharp saw.

At the end of March we finished our training and were presented with a uniform: two pairs of dungarees, three biscuit-coloured airtex shirts, a green pullover, working boots, three pairs of top stockings, a pair of breeches, a greatcoat and a stiff waterproof. Complete with new uniform, I was posted to Glendoick, near Perth, where I earned forty-eight shillings for a forty-eight hour week! Jean Macnaughton, Margaret Weir and I were soon promoted to leader girls and got an extra two and sixpence a week.

Quickly settling in to our new quarters, which were an improvement on Meiklour, we were pleased as the days lengthened and the weather improved. One of our first jobs there was to build a bridge over the burn to the camp. The men helped us and it was an excellent piece of work when finished.

On Saturdays, we sometimes went to Perth to have a look round the shops, have tea in the Windsor Tearoom and, perhaps, go to the pictures. On a good day we often walked back to camp over the hills and burns. I remember finding my first cowslips at a wee burn below a thatched cottage at Balthayock. It was a great pleasure to walk over the hills and glens around Glendoick at the weekends. Near the camp was a lovely little loch surrounded by cherry and almond trees. On our way to work up the hillside there were blaeberry bushes, bearing huge berries in the summer. Once, I found a large mushroom which I took back to camp and cooked in a frying pan borrowed from the cook.

In April and May, we saw a great many capercaillies in our wood. The cock would take off noisily from the branches and then we would discover the hen sitting quietly on eggs at the base of the tree, merging so well with the ground around that it was difficult to spot her.

Morag Shorthouse

There was a lot of Scots Pine in Pitlowie Glen, where we worked. They were easy trees to log, making it a pleasure to work with them. As Jean Macnaughton, Margaret Weir and I were tall, we often got a request to help Dunc Smith, the ganger, to load the lorry. He was a big, strapping fellow who expected us to lift these huge logs. No wonder we were ready for our dinner at night!

In the spring of 1943, Jean Macnaughton and I were asked to go to Shandford Lodge as trainers. It was a lovely house and we enjoyed the relative comfort there. Five of us shared a room, Marjory Stark (Starkie), Betty Croll, Molly Sinclair, Jean and myself. There were ten trainers in all, each responsible for the training of ten girls. Bonny Macadam, having a heavy goods license, drove one of the lorries and also taught some of the girls to drive. On the way to and from camp we sang all kinds of songs about the WTC to old tunes, producing quite a few budding artistes!

At Shandford we gained experience in many different types of forest work. Mr Allison, now Chief Instructor for WTC Scotland, even gave us marching lessons when we were invited to join a parade in Edinburgh!

It was decided to start a unit solely for women at Roughmount Wood, near Shandford and Jean and I were asked to go as forewoman and ganger respectively. Huts were soon erected: two sleeping huts, a kitchen and dining hut and separate quarters for Jean and me consisting of a small sitting room, two cubicles with beds, wash-hand basins and (luxury!) a shower.

Late in 1943 a letter arrived from Edinburgh announcing a felling competition and requesting two entrants from each camp. Jean put my name forward along with that of Mary Curran, so we had to get in a little practice as we had never felled together. The competition, with twelve pairs of girls taking part, was held near Kirriemuir We were shown the trees we had to fell, the stop watches were set and we started, with all eyes on us. Unfortunately, we did not get the first prize of a silver cup but we came second. Mr Scott from the Perth office said he would donate ten shillings to the fastest

159

snedder so off we went again and this time I won amid great hilarity and applause.

Jean and I were then offered a 'piece-work' job at Kinnordy, where we worked in Drum Wood which had a lot of nice timber: Spruce, Douglas Fir and Silver Fir. They were all full of resin bubbles that burst on hot days, leaving us very sticky, but we enjoyed working together.

The winter of 1944-45 was very severe, with heavy snowfalls and hard frosts. We had to fill basins with snow and melt it on top of the stove to give us water for washing. No vans or cars could get up the road, so one Saturday six of us set off, each carrying a pillowcase and a line for the grocer. We walked to Kirriemuir, collected the rations and managed to get back to camp without too much trouble. The kitchen staff were really glad to see us! The weather remained very cold so we were allowed to go home till the thaw set in.

When we were working in the woods, we used to get water from a wee cottage up the hill. One day, when it was my turn, the old woman gave me a strange look and said, 'Eh, ma loon, are ye no feart working wi a' they quines? Watch them well.' I laughed all the way back to the wood and when I told the others we all collapsed on the grass with mirth. I had an Eton Crop at the time and she thought I was a boy! In spite of the hard work, we had many laughs.

There were such a lot of birds and insects in the woods. We loved watching the ladybirds creeping up our arms and even got used to the ferocious-looking wood wasps, once we knew they were harmless. A great many moths and butterflies flitted around us; red and brown, blue and white. Sometimes, the flies annoyed us and often we were bitten by mosquitoes, midges and clegs. Around some of the bogs at Kinnordy there was a vivid splash of green and blue in the evenings as truly beautiful dragonflies flitted about like helicopters.

Lovely wild flowers and ferns, growing near the burns, delighted us. Beetles, spiders of every colour and many different kinds of fungus, from stink horns to red fairy umbrellas, made life in the woods interesting.

There were no roaring power saws then, just the sound of

the axe and the cross-cut saw and a shout of **'Timber!'** every now and again, followed by the swish of a falling tree.

By the late summer of 1945, quite a few girls had left to return to civilian life but some stayed on to go out to Germany to help with the clerical work involved in the clearing up and replanting of the devastated German forests. I left the WTC in November 1945 and, in January 1949, married Bill Shorthouse to whom I had written during all the war years.

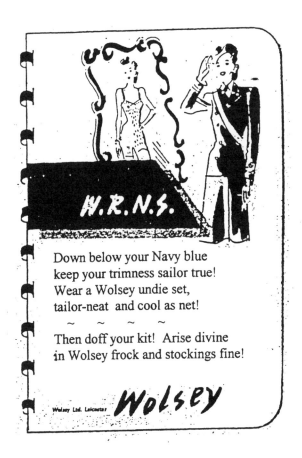

W.R.N.S.

Down below your Navy blue
keep your trimness sailor true!
Wear a Wolsey undie set,
tailor-neat and cool as net!

~ ~ ~ ~

Then doff your kit! Arise divine
in Wolsey frock and stockings fine!

Wolsey Ltd. Leicester

Wolsey

Timber!

Item No.	Possible	Ethie	Balbirnie	Glendoick	Largo	Bamff	Meikleour	Shandford	Fern
1. Laying in	10	8	5	8	10	8	7	9	8
2. Cutting Low & 5. Cleanest break	10	9	5	7	9	8	9	10	8
3. Axemanship	10	8	6	7	10	8	7	9	9
4. Direction	10	5	6	8	10	7	5	6	10
6. Snedding	10	10	9	10	10	9	7	10	10
7. Co-operation	10	8	7	8	10	8	9	7	9
8. Cross-cutting	10	10	10	10	10	9	10	6	10
9. Time	20	16	15	17	18	14	17	18	19
10. Special Points	10	8	4	8	10	5	6	8	8
TOTALS	100	82	67	83	97	76	77	83	91

The New Camp

When the Timber Corps camped at Pityoulish,
The gales around them blew,
The snow lay thick on the trees and hills,
It lay on their bedding too!

And the rain came down in buckets,
The huts were all awash,
But as they wrung out their blankets,
The Timber Corps only said 'Gosh!'

Now Mr Greig was the foreman,
A man of worth was he,
He said in his wrath, 'This will never do,
These lassies will surely dee.'

So he spoke to Mr McIver,
And he spoke to Mr Gray,
He said, with an oath, 'Move these girls from the hill,
And build them a camp straight away.'

So all the 'phones got busy,
And the wires flashed here and there,
The trees were cut down – the ground measured out –
All done with the greatest of care.

But Autumn turned to Winter,
And Xmas and New Year were past,
And the early snowdrops were withering too,
E'er the final plans were passed.

Timber!

Away up on the heights the lassies
Grew pinched and pale with cold,
And they cried in their sleep 'If we're left up here
We'll never live to grow old.'

The Boy Friends stood in nobly,
And said, 'Come to a hop,
Forget that you're cold, forget that you're tired:
We'll pick you up if you drop.'

So bravely they all struggled onward,
And lo and behold, one day
The new camp rose before them,
So neat and cosy and gay.

Now they've come to live by the Druie,
The Girls of the Timber Corps,
The Camp's come alive with khaki and green
And the place is silent no more.

So let's drink a toast to the new camp,
With peace and content reigning there,
Till the world is at peace, and true happiness reigns,
In which one and all have a share.

IMS

ANNE SHORTREED

Anne graduated from the Edinburgh College of Art in 1937. When war broke out she first joined the Women's Timber Corps and became a trainer at Park House in Aberdeenshire before going to the Anna Freud Institute in London. In 1945 she went with founding members of the post-war British Embassy to Czechoslovakia, assisting with resettlement of British women married to men of the former free Czechoslovakia.

Winning a British Council Scholarship to Prague College of Applied Arts in 1946, Anne graduated from there with a degree in Art in 1951. She then went to northern Moravia as the artist responsible for workers' portraiture, murals and illustrations for a youth newspaper for State information and publicity. After this assignment she returned to Prague where she married and continued to produce graphic work and illustrations. She also worked with the Czech radio English Department and illustrated translations of English books, including Sir Walter Scott's *Heart of Midlothian*, before returning to Scotland in 1965 to continue painting and drawing.

Anne taught in Art Departments in West Lothian secondary schools until she retired in 1980. Since then she has taught adults and private groups and continues with her own art work which she has exhibited in many towns, both in this country and abroad. Her works are also in many private collections throughout the United Kingdom, Czechoslovakia, the USA, Australia, Canada, France and Japan.

We are much indebted to Anne for the lively drawings that she has contributed to this book about the Scottish Women's Timber Corps.

Timber!

In 1990, when Bonny Macadam, along with three other former lumberjills, decided to see if there would be any interest in a reunion of wartime Women's Timber Corps members, they sat down and drew up lists of names, remembered from almost half a century before. One member of the Timber Corps had not been heard of since 1945 when, it was believed, she had gone to Prague with the British Embassy. A newspaper cutting from 1947 explained that Anne Shortreed, daughter of an Edinburgh family, was studying art in Prague and that she had designed a poster advertising the Prague Zoo. It seemed that the Shortreed family no longer lived in Edinburgh, so Bonny decided to ask her local Member of Parliament, Menzies Campbell, for some assistance. Mr Campbell tried to trace Anne through the Foreign Office but the information he had was too vague and he drew a blank there.

Undeterred, Menzies Campbell contacted the Czechoslovakian Embassy which was able to give Miss Shortreed's date of entry into Czechoslovakia, the date of her marriage and her married name, Mrs Fried. They also disclosed that Anne and her husband had moved back to Scotland and that she had been back to Czechoslovakia several times to visit relatives. From her application for a visa they were able to obtain her address.

And so Anne Shortreed and Bonny Macadam were reunited after forty-five years, thanks to some remarkable detective work by MP Menzies Campbell.

THE WOMEN'S TIMBER CORPS
IN SCOTLAND, 1942-46

Sub-Committee Report

In the twenty-third report of the Select Committee appointed to examine the National Expenditure on Defence Services the sub-committee reported on conditions of employment in the production of Home Grown Timber and, in particular, on the conditions for women. In 1941 women born in 1920 and 1921 were eligible for call-up to the Women's Auxiliary Services, which included work in the Women's Forestry Service.

At that time the labour force in the forests was largely recruited from men and women who had never done such work before. The sub-committee was much impressed with the work being done by women and they recommended that the training and employment of girls should be expanded as much as possible. The girls were paid on time rates and as it happened that they sometimes worked alongside men on piece-work it was suggested that the possibility of introducing piece-work rates for women should be seriously considered.

It was also agreed that it was necessary to improve the facilities for recreation. It was noted that each camp had a recreation room but, with the exception of the Newfoundlanders' camps, they were almost bare of any means of recreation. The sub-committee members were glad that £10 had been allotted to each camp for the purchase of wireless, gramophone and books. They recommended that some form of transport be made available to take employees to the nearest town should they wish to go to the cinema or a dance, as the Army did for the Canadians.

With regard to bedding it was learnt that sheets were not

provided for the men, which raised problems of cleanliness! Washing arrangements were inevitably primitive in some of the more outlying places but stoves should be installed to heat the water and blankets should be washed with reasonable frequency! It was deemed essential to keep a locked store in which blankets could be kept to prevent unordered and casual exchange of dirty and new bedding.

Status of Girls

The question of the status of girls was considered and, as it was agreed that they were carrying out their work in an efficient manner, the sub-committee recommended that the Service should be expanded. The terms should be made as attractive as possible to encourage recruits. Comparisons with the Women's Land Army were made and the sub-committee did not doubt that the added pride which would accompany belonging to such a service would encourage the girls to conform to any regulations laid down for them.

Forestry girls would probably live at a much greater distance from home than the girls of the Land Army so consideration was given to the expense entailed in returning home for holidays. Members of the Land Army living more than twenty miles from home were entitled to one free return ticket home after each six months of service so the sub-committee recommended that forestry girls be entitled to a similar system of travelling allowances.

The Women's Forestry Service of the Forestry Commission was then organised on the same lines as the Women's Land Army until the formation of the Women's Timber Corps in 1942.

From the first of May, 1942, by Government Decree, all unmarried women born in 1918 and 1919 were required to register for National Service either in the services or in civilian occupations which comprised Munitions, Agriculture, Forestry and other industries connected with the war effort. In the event, girls younger than seventeen, women over fifty and some married women also volunteered and were accepted if physically fit. The response was terrific and the option for service, particularly in the resuscitated Land Army and the newly formed Women's Timber Corps, astonishing. They came from all walks of life and were shop girls, typists, hairdressers, students and office girls. Did they realise what lay ahead? For some it must have been a traumatic experience.

Picture a young city woman being suddenly transported from the cushioned existence of office or shop life, their safe home life, to the rigours of perhaps hutted accommodation, the strange experience of unknown country life and, in the case of the Land Army, the petrifying intimacy with wild animals: rabbits, hares, geese, turkeys, cows, bulls and horses – even, in some cases, the farmer himself! In the case of those who opted for the WTC, the rough and tumble of timber operations, the grime and dirt, the petrifying cold in the winter handling logs with frozen hands, spartan accommodation and food rations, must all have been quite daunting.

Training Centres

Training centres were set up and, when the first set of recruits had been trained, some of these girls became trainers themselves. Marjory Stark, Mary Mitchell, Jean Macnaughton, Morag Mackenzie and Bonny Macadam were among those at Shandford Lodge, near Brechin. The other main training centre was at Park House, Drumoak, in Aberdeenshire, where our illustrator, Anne Shortreed, was a trainer. In the first week of the course recruits were introduced to the four main sections of timber work: felling, cross-cutting, snedding and driving tractors or lorries. The girls had one month in which to decide if they felt suited to the work, while the Department retained the right to decide in that time whether the recruits were likely to succeed. Once launched on the work, only five per cent applied to leave.

A report in the Bon Accord in May 1943 showed pictures of WTC girls doing 'keep fit' exercises to help to toughen them up for their work in the woods. It points out that the Timber

Timber!

Corps needed many more girls for the healthy outdoor life and that the response from the North-East corner was surprisingly small compared to other parts of the country. The reporter was visiting Park House, Drumoak, home of the late Sir Robert and Lady Williams.

At a press conference at St Andrews House, Edinburgh, Councillor J.J. Robertson, senior Labour Officer for Scotland to the Ministry of Supply, said that former shop girls were proving to be excellent 'lumber Jills' from the point of view of stamina, as they were accustomed, in their job, to standing for long hours. There had been some difficulty in breaking down prejudice against using women's labour, especially among the older timber merchants, but his experience in visiting camps had convinced him of the suitability of using girls to fell trees. Mr Robertson also noted that there was an amazing change in physique in the girls in a very short time! Many members also commented on the size of their muscles after a month of felling trees! He said he had asked a girl, working zealously in a snow blizzard, why she was working in such appalling conditions and she replied 'We want to show you men that we can do this job!'

'Production figures', said Mr Robertson, 'compared very favourably with those when men did all the work.' He added that an effort was to be made to extend the recreational facilities in the following winter. Wireless, gramophone and books were already provided and inter-camp social evenings organised but transport remained the biggest difficulty, due to petrol rationing.

As regards food, a camp committee was formed of the supervisor, the cook and three other girls. The welfare officer for the area examined the menus to see that the food was of good quality and that the meals provided a balanced diet.

The camps were organised for twenty to forty girls and the whole cost of living in these camps was never more than £1 a week and sometimes as low as ten shillings. It is difficult to believe these figures now.

It is interesting to note that in 1942 the number enlisting for the Women's Timber Corps was 1100, rising to 1400 in 1943,

1040 in 1944 and 450 in 1945. The Corps was disbanded in August 1946.

Fatalities

There were few recorded fatalities but one tragic accident took place at Mount Wood, Aberuthven, near Perth. Ethel Torbet had only been in the WTC for five months when she was tragically killed during tree-felling operations on March 11th 1942. There was an inquest in Perth Sheriff Court following the accident when lumberjills gave evidence. The foreman at the lumber camp said there were fifty-five people in the working party in Mount Wood and, of these, twenty-two were lumberjills. They were considered to be experienced in the woods, their duties being mainly felling, cross-cutting and snedding. Evidence showed that on the morning of the accident a tree was being felled by two woodcutters who had shouted the warning '**Timber!**' as a signal to the girls to keep clear. However, while they were working the saw had jammed and two girls and a man had gone to push the tree in the direction it was meant to fall. As they were pushing, the tree snapped at the roots and began to fall the wrong way. The girls ran for safety but Miss Torbet ran in the wrong direction and, to the distress of her companions, was crushed by the tree. The witnesses were of the opinion that the tree fell in the wrong direction because of the twisted nature of its roots which was only apparent after the tree fell. The foreman repeated that the most important instruction in felling is the shout of '**Timber!**', but agreed with the judge that it would render this type of accident less likely if the workers were to stand behind a tree about to fall and not at the side.

Another fatal accident happened in Kingussie in June, 1942, after which an inquiry into the cause of death was held in Inverness Sheriff Court.

Olive Clarke had been employed in the Home Grown Timber Department of the Ministry of Supply at Kingussie Railway Station in checking all timber sent from there by the nearby Newfoundland Forestry Unit. Sven Hansen, also

171

engaged in checking wood, said that he and Miss Clarke were standing at No. 2 loading bank watching a lorry reversing towards them. It gave a sudden spurt when it was about twenty feet away and he called to Miss Clarke to look out. It was too late and the lorry struck her, causing her to fall between the railway wagon and the buffers. She died the following day. The Sheriff thought the reason for the accident might well have been that the driver's foot had slipped from the brake to the accelerator and a verdict of accidental death was returned.

Summary

To summarise, timber was important to the war effort as it was used for pit-props in the coal mines, telegraph poles for use at home, on the beaches and in the desert campaigns, training planes, railway sleepers to keep the lines of communication open for troops and munitions, landing decks for the beaches, charcoal for making gunpowder and we must not forget that it was used for making coffins for the gallant people who laid down their lives so that we who remained would be free from the tyranny of Nazi Germany.

Also, we must remember the contribution of the girls who took on the burden of increasing paper-work, an invaluable service to the foremen who were then free to direct work in the woods and saw-mills.

PRODUCTION

What precisely did the WTC do in the production of timber? The answer is contained in the one word 'everything' – everything that men did and just as skilfully after brief training and practice. Their adaptation to the skills was quite astonishing and a lesson to the men! They felled and snedded trees with rare abandon, cross-cut to specified lengths, dragged with horses and tractors to a pick-up point then loaded on to timber bogies and hauled by tractor to propping yards or, in the case of sawn timber, to the saw-mill. All very arduous work and muscle-testing! At the propping yard a team cross-cut the timber into pit props of various diameters and stacked them in alleys according to diameter and length. The space between the alleys was sufficiently wide for a lorry to operate so, when orders were received, the lorry team, driver and checker, loaded the lorry with the required size of prop and drove to the railway station where wagons had already been arranged with the Station Master by the Operations Foreman. Both girls loaded the wagons and then the checker did the consigning in the Station Office.

WTC at Auchterblair

The history of one particular propping yard in my Strathspey District is worth recording.

The name of the unit was Auchterblair and the scene of operation was Carr Wood in Carrbridge. The Unit was worked entirely by the WTC under the supervision of that splendid and highly efficient Operations Foreman, Peter Mackenzie, to whom I owe so much for his co-operation in creating such a viable Unit and with whom I remain in contact.

Timber!

When I was transferred from Acquisitions in the North Division based in Inverness to a Speyside Division, I was District Officer for the South District which stretched from Broomhill near Dulnain Bridge to Dalwhinnie. There were ten production units in the district, some with one or two saw-mills, each under very co-operative and highly efficient Operations Foremen and each with a goodly complement of WTC. Sadly, most of the Foremen are now deceased. The Divisional Officer was the late Mr MacIver, who was highly efficient on the administrative side of timber operations.

When I first met him, I was instructed to make a tour of the whole District and report back to him with my findings. It was obvious when I visited each unit and covered each operation meticulously that the whole District had been sadly mismanaged since Operations commenced. When I told him so, as diplomatically as possible, and said that if I was to be responsible for production in the District I intended to stop all felling until the backlog of extraction and haulage to propping yards had been completed, he did not, as I feared, have an apoplectic fit, but confessed that he was very concerned about the WTC unit at Carrbridge where the production of pit props was at a very low level. I promised to treat this Unit as a priority and in view of the fact that I lived in Carrbridge and, fortunately, so did the Operations Manager, Peter Mackenzie, there was plenty of opportunity to discuss every angle of the operation. Peter, being otherwise fully occupied, it seemed to me, after studying the girls at work, my best way of getting the feel of the job from their viewpoint was to work alongside them for a few days but I could not do this without the approval of the 'Old Man'. At first he could not follow the logic of what I proposed and, in any case, he regarded it as rather undignified for a District Officer to descend to that level simply to prove a point. However, I finally persuaded him that it was the best thing to do in the interests of increased production.

Firstly, there was nothing wrong with the axes and, in any case, the girls were quite capable of keeping them sharp themselves. Dealing with cross-cut saws, however, is a skilled job and was difficult for them at first. This problem was solved by taking the saws regularly to a local woodcutter for attention. One girl was taught to deal with a garron, a highland pony, for dragging trees to the edge of the wood where they were cut into suitable lengths before loading on to a trailer for hauling to the propping yard where two girls manned a portable saw-bench and cut the logs into pit props. The props were loaded on to wheelbarrows which were trundled down the alleys and then stacked according to length and diameter at the small end. I thought this was too laborious and primitive and suggested laying light railway tracks and acquiring bogies to run the props up and down the alleys. Peter was full of enthusiasm but I cautioned that we must get all this done on the quiet and present the 'Old Man' with a fait accompli. Unfortunately, however, the 'OM' happened to need a breath of fresh air out of the office and motored round by Auchterblair. I was elsewhere at the time. Apparently he was in a fine rage when he observed a light railway in the making and ordered Peter to leave forthwith. Peter, of course, had no option and when I arrived home a message awaited me to appear in Head Office next morning.

When asked to explain the 'tom-foolery' at Auchterblair I produced all the arguments in the book about the benefits that would accrue but he refused to listen and I got the roasting of my life. I was told in no uncertain terms that he didn't want 'any of my ridiculous, expensive ideas in his Division', not another ha'penny must be spent and what had already been done must be dismantled. I had no option but to say, tongue in cheek, 'Very well, not another ha'penny will be spent but I think you are making a big mistake.' I went straight out to Peter and, after recounting my carpeting, fumed, 'You know and I know that if this propping yard is set out the way we envisage production will increase. If that old Buzzard thinks he can stand in the way of progress, he is making a big mistake.' I explained, however, that orders were orders so we would have to work on the quiet and without incurring expense. I suggested to him that the work could be carried out in the evenings and asked if he would be willing to work with me? His answer was exactly what I had antici-pated. Peter was full of enthusiasm. So Peter and I worked like beavers for several nights laying the tracks. All went well until we had to curve the rails. We had no means of obtaining a 'Jim Crowe' for bending them and had to resort to placing them between standing trees, hitching the ends to a little Bristol Caterpillar and pulling like mad, with Peter at the helm and I judging the moment when the curve appeared correct. When flames shot out of the exhaust I shouted, 'Keep her going, Peter. Keep her going and never mind the flames!' It worked and we eventually succeeded in getting two rails curved in the same plane. This was no easy task so, after asking around, we acquired a 'Jim Crowe' from Dulnain Bridge. Peter had a little bit of fun with this. He instructed Nancy, the Auchterblair driver, to go to Dulnain Bridge and bring back Jim Crowe. All innocence, Nancy went to the Operations Foreman there and told him she had come to pick up Jim. She took a long time to live down that episode! When the work was completed, the primitive method of barrowing the props was replaced by the smooth running bogies. The saw-bench was cleared more quickly and everybody was happy. Piece-work was introduced and, without having to tax themselves unduly, the girls were able to add an addi-tional £2 to £3 to their wage packet which, at the time, meant a great deal. Production rapidly increased and, to my aston-ishment and delight, it exceeded similar work carried out by men at other units.

There was a sequel. Some time after the re-organisation at Carrbridge and the introduction of the light railway the units were visited by Sir Samuel Strang Stark, Sir James Calder, a timber merchant, and others from the Ministry of Supply, Home Grown Timber Production Department. When they came to Auchterblair, Sir James Calder commented to the 'Old Man', 'By Jove, M., I notice a tremendous improvement in the system here.' 'Yes, Sir James,' said the 'OM' and quite blatantly added, much to my amusement, 'I felt that I had to change things and decided that this was the most efficient way.' Afterwards, he never once referred to the railtrack or the phenomenal rise in production!

However, when I met him years later, working in Pitlochry, I realised that he had a tremendous sense of humour. Perhaps he had been quietly laughing at a young, rather serious, District Officer at Auchterblair!

I have written at length about the Unit at Auchterblair because, being all WTC, it was quite unique in the whole Speyside Division, but it should not detract from the enormous contribution of the members under: Roddy Urquhart at Balvattan and Broomhill, Jim at Tomdhu and Loch Vaa, John Ross at Inchriach and Tromie Bridge, Jim Greig at Rothiemurchus and Jim Rose at Glentruim.

Production

During the war Forestry Commission forests in Britain produced more than 50 million cubic feet of timber but ninety per cent of all timber used in the war effort came from private estates, requisitioned for the supply of pit-props on which the mining industry relied.

It was estimated that from the outbreak of war till December 1945 a total of 65 million cubic feet of sawn mining timber and around 100 million cubic feet of pit props were produced by Scottish woodlands. Some land owners have never replanted but others made sure that natural regeneration took place by insisting on some trees being left standing.

One of the major problems in timber felling is the disposal of waste products such as sawdust and slabs or backs. The latter were often sold as firewood to supplement the coal ration but the transportation of sawdust was expensive and, as the railways were already under strain, the sub-committee on National Expenditure suggested that research into the use of waste products should be pressed forward with utmost speed. In Strathspey we used sawdust for bottoming paths.

Canadian Forestry Corps production of sawn timber in Scotland reached almost one million cubic feet and their output of round mining timber totalled 222,000 tonnes by the end of the war. The CFC made use of logs from sources other than its own fellings. This was particularly true in Strathspey where the Newfoundlanders, along with the Women's Timber Corps, were supplying around sixty-five per cent of the total used in the Abernethy saw-mill in December 1943. Out of a total area of 232,000 acres the CFC helped to clear 68,000 acres which, of course, contributed to the urgency for re-afforestation in Scotland after the war.

In 1943, a White Paper proposed that, in a post-war policy, the aim should be five million acres of commercial timber, most of which would be the responsibility of the Forestry Commission, with private estates also being encouraged to replant areas which had been requisitioned for the war effort.

A training scheme for forest workers was introduced in 1946 and between then and 1948 one hundred and sixty one graduates came out of forestry schools, two of which were in Scotland at Benmore and Glentress.

In Caithness, on the northernmost estate owned by the Forestry Commission, work in the forests and nurseries went on steadily with the greatest problem being the distance of one hundred miles between Borgie and the tractor maintenance engineer, my father-in-law, Kenneth Mackenzie.

Reafforestation

By 1949 it was apparent that afforestation was so important in Britain that a decision to build 'forest villages' was taken by the Forestry Commission, in the hope that it would bring people back to the rural areas they had left for war service. Glenbranter and Ae Village were two such in Scotland. Some former members of the Women's Timber Corps, who had married foresters, lived happily in these newly constructed communities.

DISBANDMENT AND DISENCHANTMENT

In 1946 the Women's Timber Corps was disbanded and the Government of the day acknowledged their contribution to the war effort with a few faint appreciative remarks which might have been more appropriate if translated into something more tangible such as a gratuity of some sort, if only to replace, in some cases, civilian clothes and footwear the women wore before being kitted out with uniform.

After the War?

What did the Timber Corps members do when the war was over and the male foresters came home? Some continued to work for the Forestry Commission, especially in research; many married, some going as far afield as Australia, America, Canada and Newfoundland; many returned to the jobs which they had left in the hands of married women, some working part-time, in shops, offices, hairdressing salons and restaurants; and some went to Germany with the Control Commission to act as secretaries and clerkesses for the Forest Officers, like myself, who went to oversee reparations in the German forests.

In February 1946 I received confirmation of my appointment in the North German Timber Control with the Control Commission for Germany (British Element) to help with reafforestation in a countryside devastated by war.

A warning was given to us to expect a different mode of life from that at home. Trunk road and rail services had been partly restored but we were told that accommodation might be rather primitive. Could it have been worse than some WTC units endured in their service? Food was scarce, though not more so than at home, and in the clubs for CCG and Service ranks we could expect a good meal for 3/-, whilst whisky and gin were 6d. a tot, when available! We would not be able to supplement our rations from provisions shops as there were none. However, we were permitted to go shooting and fishing, in the appropriate season, to supplement the larder. This we did.

There was plenty of entertainment in the shape of cinemas and concerts and, in the towns, dances were held regularly. Some ex-WTC members enjoyed a good social life.

The minor roads were in poor condition in 1946 though the main routes were used and maintained by the Services. However, this did not prevent a group of us, with a love of the hills, from exploring the countryside and climbing in the Harz mountains, south of Hanover. Some of the towns were completely razed to the ground and it was an impressive sight to witness the Germans at work rebuilding their home towns and cities. Those of us who had had protected occupations in the war were appalled by the conditions. The radio bulletins and newspapers could not have prepared anyone for the actuality of the devastation.

In the forest I had a group of Estonians who were great workers, in addition to being a most interesting and cultured people. Many subsequently came to this country and tried to find work as conditions at home were not easy for them. I remember writing a reference for one who was willing to try his hand at any work to establish himself in this country. They were referred to as 'displaced persons' or, popularly, 'DPs'.

The German forest workers did not care for us at first but soon realised that we were there to help them back to some degree of normality. I corresponded with the foreman for some time after coming home and he was grateful to receive conifer seeds from me to try in the nursery. As time went by his letters developed a more positive tone and it appeared that the extensive damage in the forests was improving with a programme of planting and sowing. Both German and Estonian workers were gifted with their hands and I own several, beautifully carved, wooden objects which they presented to me on my departure. I finished my work in Germany in March 1947.

A Record of the Women's Timber Corps?

A small booklet, author unnamed, with the title 'Meet the Members', published in 1946, contains much useful information about the Corps and some reminiscences by the members. The foreword by Sir Gerald Lenanton, who was Director of the Home Grown Timber Department, Ministry of Supply, expressed his appreciation of all the Corps had endured and achieved in the production of timber. Unfortunately, the book is out of print, although it is available in some libraries and a copy was given to the National Museum in Edinburgh by a former member.

I have no doubt that Marjory Stark would have been only too keen to give her permission to have her article on 'Felling' reprinted in this account of the WTC. Sadly, she died before writing her story for the book but, as I know she was held in the highest regard by all the girls in her care, I am sure they would wish to see her name amongst the contributors. There is also a poem about Rothiemurchus by a member with initials IMS, in which I feature!

Admittedly, there was a 'March Past' of the Corps in the major cities and towns which received some press publicity but, by and large, the public was unaware of the Timber Corps. There was a very well attended reunion, arranged by Doreen Butler, Lochgilphead, in the Kelvin Hall in Glasgow in 1974 to which Land Army and Timber Corps ladies came from far and wide to meet with friends whom they had not seen since Disbandment. Much, but not enough, was said and written about the WLA because of the heroic work they did on the land, helping to feed the Nation in times of serious shortage. Also, south of the border, members have been more articulate than in Scotland and a number of excellent books have been published depicting the arduous work of the members, interspersed with hilarious recollections of the social side of their lives.

Timber!

In the literary sense, Mavis Danks (née Williams), with whom I had an exchange of correspondence, has done sterling work for the WTC with her book 'Lumber Jill'. Published in 1994, it is not only revealing but also very amusing in parts. Much is due to that indomitable and enduring lady Bonny Macadam, who has helped to keep the memory of the WTC alive. At considerable personal expense and time in a very busy life, she contacted ex-members and arranged reunions in the Queen's Hotel, Perth in 1990, 1991 and 1992 that were highly successful and provided a number with the opportunity to meet again with old friends they hadn't seen since Disbandment. These were very jolly occasions which I was privileged to attend. For the fiftieth anniversary in 1992 Bonny received a message of good wishes from Queen Elizabeth The Queen Mother to be passed on to all who attended the reunion.

Many of the letters I received mention a Benevolent Fund. In 1959, the Royal Scottish Agricultural Benevolent Institution was approached by the Department of Agriculture and Fisheries of Scotland, who proposed to hand over the administration of the Scottish Women's Land Army Welfare and Benevolent Fund. This was done in 1961, when Lord Airlie, a Trustee of the Institution, accepted the Fund, agreeing that it would continue to be applied for the benefit of ex-members of the WLA, who might be in need of assistance. This, therefore, included members of the Women's Timber Corps. The fund is very small but still disburses money to those in need.

I was interested to see in a letter to Marjory Stark, dated 20th November 1945, that Dorothy Simpson, Chief Officer, WTC, said she was unable to visit Bowmont Camp that week as her time was largely taken up with meetings, including a meeting of the Benevolent Fund Committee.

Conclusion

To conclude this brief and, I'm afraid, totally inadequate account of a Corps that contributed so much, albeit mostly unrecognised, to the war effort, I am left with a deep sense of

Disbandment and Disenchantment

regret that I did not keep a diary and attempt to put all that transpired on record. Time dims memory and much has been lost as a result. It has been a frustrating and time-consuming exercise trying to squeeze old records from Government Departments. I have also to confess with deep regret that writing a history just never occurred to me until I became conscience stricken when I was invited to the 1990 Reunion in Perth and encountered so many of the splendid ladies who had survived the years, many of whom looked as though they could still swing an axe and log a tree if the need arose! You must judge for yourselves, Ladies, to what extent this inadequate ramble has done you justice.

Affleck Gray, FSA (Scotland)

THE FORGOTTEN TIMBER CORPS

This poem, written by one of the men who worked with the WTC, was found by a member from Lewis and expresses the view that the valuable work of the Timber Corps was not recognised as it should have been:

When days of peace come back again and warriors sheath
    their swords,
There'll be cheers for them, and handshakes, and kindly
    spoken words.
The soldier, and the sailor, and the air force boys as well,
Will tell of mighty combats, of guns, of bombs and hell.
They'll praise the gallant A.T.S. who manned the ack-ack
    guns,
Who, side by side with soldier lads, drove off the bombing
    Huns.
The sailor lads, with pride, will tell of work done by the
    W.R.N.S.
And the pilot speaks of W.A.A.F.s who guide the bombers
    home again.
There'll be praise for every service, and medals by the score,
For all except that noble band, the forgotten Timber Corps.
The one and only service that seldom reached the news
Because they never manned a gun or called in bombing crews.
Though, each day wet with honest sweat they toil for long,
    long hours
Regardless of the blazing sun or the soaking, drenching
    showers.

The poem goes on to point out that the mining industry, on which the whole industrial life of the country depended, was

The Forgotten Timber Corps

itself dependent on an adequate supply of pit props from the
girls of the Timber Corps:

> So that gallant band of lassies, with grim determination,
> Axed and felled, sawed and cut, the wood that saved the
>   nation.
> So, let it ever be remembered, in the days that lie ahead,
> When they're showering all the glory on heroes live and dead,
> How the wheels of our great industries were once so nearly
>   stopped
> Due to lack of coal from mines that cried aloud for props,
> For props that are forthcoming, and coming now galore.
> I ask you, please, now one and all, salute the Timber Corps.

REUNIONS

In 1989 an item appeared in the Craigie Column of the Dundee *Courier* asking if anyone was familiar with the wartime Women's Timber Corps. The floodgates opened and many former members wrote in to the *Courier* with their memories. Chris Renton (née Lamont) had been speaking to a group of ladies about the plants and trees of the Bible and, in passing, mentioned that she had been in the Timber Corps during the war. At the end of the meeting a member of the group said that she had seen a piece in the *Courier* that very day about the WTC. Chris worked for a timber merchant in Musselburgh after her training at Shandford Lodge and had stayed in private digs, unlike many girls who had lived in camps.

A member from Friockham remembers driving the Bedford three-tonner on a Saturday evening to convey girls to Brechin, Forfar or RAF Kinnell. She remembers that, although the lorry had a canvas canopy, some girls always elected to sit with their legs dangling over the tailboard. On one occasion the farmer at Findowrie had been cleaning out the byres and the road was awash. The legs received the full impact!

These recollections in the Dundee *Courier* prompted Bonny Macadam and three friends, Jean Buntin, Mary Shepherd and Jean Smith, to consider the idea of a reunion. They decided to test the water by putting forward the idea in the Craigie Column, which had started the correspondence. By December 1989, it was obvious that there was great enthusiasm for the idea and so Bonny and her team started the mammoth task of contacting people they had not met for forty-five years or more. The response was, in fact, so overwhelming that a tentative date of the spring of 1990 had to be postponed till the autumn of that year. The reunion, in the Queen's Hotel in Perth, on 19th September 1990, was a huge success, with lumberjills coming from as far afield as Australia, America and Canada to share their memories. The Queen Mother sent her greetings to the members and her good wishes for the success of the occasion. Bonny said that one hundred and sixty people attended and, since the first item appeared in the Craigie Column, she had spoken to no fewer than two hundred and eighty former WTC members. Along with the ladies at the reunion were some brave men!: Bob Allison, Chief Instructor for Scotland, Alan Gairns, head of one of the camps, and Affleck Gray, Acquisitions Officer for the north of Scotland and subsequently District Officer in Strathspey.

Listening to the recollections of the girls, it was obvious that, while they shared a great pride in the work they had done, they also felt that it had been largely unrecognised. The germ of an idea to collect and preserve the memories then began to take shape in Affleck's mind.

The Fife-based timber company, James Donaldson and Sons, helped the ladies to celebrate in style. Instrumental in setting up the drinks for the toast was George Donaldson who had been told of the reunion and felt the ladies deserved recognition. Mr Donaldson's uncle, Victor Donaldson, was president of the Scottish Timber Merchants' and Sawmillers' Association from 1936 till 1938 and became an area officer on Timber Control, responsible for allocating stocks for civilian use. After lunch the Forestry Commission sent a mini-bus to take any interested members to Kinnoull Hill to observe for themselves modern methods at close quarters. Most of them decided it was very noisy compared to the old methods!

In 1991 the reunion was repeated by popular demand and even more former members came along, this time armed with photographs to jog memories.

As a result of the response to the reunions in 1990 and 1991, Bonny decided to start planning for the fiftieth anniversary in 1992. Again she wrote to the Queen Mother and again received a reply with good wishes. Bonny revealed that

Timber!

Dorothy Kidd, of the Scottish Ethnological Archive was planning an exhibition at the Scottish Agricultural Museum at Ingliston for the 1992 season and was collecting stories, documents and artefacts for the Archive of the National Museum of Scotland. Already she had acquired a WTC uniform along with various tools and a fifty-year-old axe, belonging to Bonny Macadam.

The reunions brought together many friends who had lost touch in the intervening years and they all paid tribute to the enthusiasm of Bonny Macadam in devoting so much of her time to organising these happy events in the Queen's Hotel in Perth.

Unfortunately, Affleck Gray was unable to complete the series of recollections but it is hoped that the wait for them to appear has not been too long!

REFERENCES

Newspapers:

The Scotsman
The Glasgow Herald
The Inverness Courier
The Perthshire Advertiser
The Daily Express
The Badenoch Record
The Dundee Courier and Advertiser
The Bon Accord

Images of War: British Posters, 1939–45 – Public Record
    Office
The Posters that Won the War – Derek Nelson
The Land Army Handbook – W.E. Shelwell-Cooper
The Forestry Commission Slasher
*National Expenditure – 23rd Report – Home Grown Timber
    Production*
*Meet the Members – A Record of the Timber Corps of the
    Women's Land Army* – published in 1946